Blaming Children

Blaming Children

Youth Crime, Moral Panic and the Politics of Hate

Bernard Schissel

Fernwood Publishing • Halifax

Dedication

to all our children

Editing: Douglas Beall
Cover painting: "Cross My Heart, Hope to Die" by Marie Lannoo
Photo of cover painting: AK Photos, Saskatoon
Design and production: Beverley Rach
Printed and bound in Canada by: Hignell Printing Limited

Fernwood Publishing is grateful for the permission granted to reprint photos and copyright material used in this publication.

A publication of:
Fernwood Publishing
Box 9409, Station A
Halifax, Nova Scotia
B3K 5S3

Fernwood Publishing Company Limited gratefully acknowledges the financial support of the Ministry of Canadian Heritage and the Nova Scotia Department of Education and Culture.

Canadian Cataloguing in Publication Data

Schissel Bernard, 1950–

Blaming Children.

Includes bibliographical references.
ISBN 1-895686-83-0

1. Juvenile delinquency -- Canada. 2. Juvenile delinquency -- Canada -- Public opinion. 3. Mass media and public opinion -- Canada. 4. Youth in mass media -- Canada. 5. Public opinion -- Canada. I. Title.

HV9108.S34 1997   364.36'0971   C97-950032-X

First printing: May 1997
Second printing: July 1998
Third printing: July 1999
Fourth printing: July 2002

Contents

Acknowledgements

I am indebted to many people for their encouragement and assistance with this book. First, I wish to express my gratitude to my colleagues in the Department of Sociology at the University of Saskatchewan for their support, and to the University of Saskatchewan Office of Research Services Publication Fund. I am indebted, as well, to the Social Sciences and Humanities Research Council of Canada (grant number 41-095-1532). I wish to acknowledge my appreciation of the John Howard Society of Saskatoon for its commitment to helping young offenders and for its commitment to socio-legal research. I would like to thank my research assistants, Kristina Shimmons and Lauren Eisler, for their competence and dedication. Many thanks to Carolyn Carey for her interest in this work and her generous input. I would also like to express my gratitude to Errol Sharpe and the staff of Fernwood Publishing for their support and their commitment to relevant scholarly work. It has, indeed, been a pleasure working with Wayne Antony on this project, and I am grateful to him for his insights, expertise and academic competence. I would also like to thank Chris McCormick for his thoughtful and constructive reading of the manuscript.

Variations of two chapters have appeared before in print. Some of the materials from Chapter 3 appear in the *Journal of Social Justice*, forthcoming in 1997 under the title of "Youth Crime, Moral Panics, and the News: The Conspiracy Against the Marginalized in Canada." As well, some of the material from Chapter 2 appeared under the title "Post-Critical Criminology and Moral Panics: Deconstructing the Conspiracy Against Youth" in *Post Critical Criminology,* edited by Thomas O'Reilly Fleming and published by Prentice-Hall in 1996.

Lastly, I would like to thank my sons Nathan and Matthew for their youthful spirit and for making me laugh; and, most importantly, Wendy, whose unwavering support, editorial ability and intellect have made this project a joy.

Preface

This work is the result of two realities I have been forced to confront: one a result of my academic research and the other a result of being a father. The first is that, despite claims made by the UN that Canada is a more desirable country to live in than any other, we incarcerate more children per capita than any other industrialized nation, including the United States. The second, more personal reality is that several times my children have experienced the mistrust and animosity that adults hold for teenagers, for no apparent reason. My elder son, in his early teenage years, was often confronted in stores by clerks who, at best, watched every move he made and, at worst, asked him to leave if he was not going to buy something. I have discussed this with parents of other teenagers; their children's experiences have been similar. Children, in general, are not allowed to "be" in retail establishments, despite the fact that they are consumers and purchasers and that many stores depend on the patronage of children and teenagers. This reality for kids is compounded if they are poorly dressed, members of a visible minority or have unconventional body adornments, including unusual hairstyles and jewellery.

This book is an attempt to understand the origins of the fear and hatred of children, and the personal and collective emotions that allow us to treat all children as dangerous and allow and encourage our courts to incarcerate children at alarmingly high rates. After you read this book, I would ask you, the reader, to be cognizant of the signs of hatred, especially in the news and entertainment industry, but also in the world of politics. The attack on children has become good business and good politics. Almost without exception, election platforms from parties of all political philosophies contain promises to get tough on kids. It is as if children have become the new enemy of the state. They are easy to attack because they are disenfranchised and because they have very few avenues of redress. They are, in essence, the perfect scapegoats.

Chapter 1

The Study
of the Hatred of Children

A crescendo of anxious voices lamented the proliferation of the poor and unproductive in the towns and villages of England. Moralists constantly complained about the swarms of idle and dissipated young people who were not being contained within the system of household discipline—the system on which, most people believed, social stability depended. Stability in the state, Tudor preachers never tired of reminding their congregations, rested on stability in the family. (Underdown 1992:11–12)

Crime and Power

Whether Canadians like to admit it or not, Canada's war on crime, like the war on crime in many other countries and in other eras, is quickly becoming a war against youth. From varying proposals to reintroduce the death penalty for young killers to the implementation of mandatory boot camps for all young offenders, Canadian society is embarking on a crusade to increase punishment for children, ostensibly in the hopes of curbing crime. The focal point for this law and order campaign is the Young Offenders Act (YOA). Critics of the Act argue that it is too lenient, that youth are not deterred because of the soft punishments it allots in favour of excessive human rights provisions, and that the Act releases adolescent dangerous offenders into society to become adult offenders.

The law-and-order mindset in Canada and many other countries seems to stand in contradistinction to the overall principles of Canada's Young Offenders Act: that prevention and rehabilitation are constructive and that punishment and criminalization are ultimately destructive to the young offender and to the society. The Act, as a progressive, libertarian and compassionate approach to youth, attempts: to use community-based, non-carceral alternatives to formal punishment; to provide short-term maximum sentences for even the most dangerous offenders; to minimize labelling through the ensurance of anonymity through publication bans; and to provide that the civil rights of the young offender are met through adequate legal and parental representation in court. Fiscal realities being what they are, however, the goals of the YOA remain unmet in many respects. Programs and organization systems that were supposed to replace the formal justice system are poorly realized, and police and court officials are left with little alternative but to use the formal legal code in ministering to young offenders. The state's inability to support the spirit and the intent of the YOA has given right-wing political movements ample fodder for their "we told you so" agenda. With the rise in the number of "street kids" (which is certainly a social and political problem and not a criminological phenomenon) and a profusion of highly publicized violent crimes committed by youth, the "war on young offenders" is a cause celebre that politicians seem unable to resist.

I argue in this book that we are on the verge of an acute "moral panic" in this country that, if allowed to continue, will result in the indictment of all adolescents, and especially those who are marginalized and disadvantaged. The end result will be the continuing scapegoating of youth for political purposes and, as is the irony of punishment, the alienation of a more uncompromising and disaffiliated youth population. It is not a new insight to say that increasing punishment greatly increases the likelihood of violence and alienation. Despite the political rhetoric to the contrary, we do not collectively consider children our most valuable resource. In fact, we consider them one of our most dangerous threats.

Our collective disintegrating faith in the children in our society is the focus of this book. I explain the nature and the extent of the moral panic by discussing the role of the media and its affiliations with information/political systems, with its readers and viewers and with corporate Canada. The current political pastime of "blaming children" for all social evils is placed in the context of changing national and local agendas. I contend that public panics are predictable in that they have little to do with a criminogenic reality and much to do with the economic and political context in which they arise. Furthermore, crime panics are targeted at vulnerable and marginal people. In fact, a critical analysis of media coverage brings us to a particular political and moral position: public perception of the seriousness of crime is largely a matter of race, real estate (incorporating class and area) and family constitution. I would argue further that the panic that vilifies children is a coordinated and calculated attempt to nourish the ideology that supports a society stratified on the bases of race, class and gender, and that the war on kids is part of the state-capital mechanism that continually reproduces an oppressive social and economic order (Hall et al. 1978; Iyengar and Kinder 1987; Herman and Chomsky 1988).

Ironically, Canada is prepared to ignore the reality that there has been little real increase in serious youth crimes; that participation rates in criminal activities are relatively stable; that youth crime is comprised mostly of petty, unthinking acts; and that the increase recorded in official rates of youth criminal behaviour is the result of increased arrest rates and the zero-tolerance mentality of the courts. That does not mean that there are no habitual young offenders, some of whom are dangerous. Most Canadian cities are confronted with high-risk youth, many of whom are "on the street" and vulnerable to victimization and exploitation by adults. Such youth often retaliate aggressively. Although habitual and potentially dangerous offenders are a small minority, only their activities and characteristics seem to inform the moral panic debates. And their own victimization and disadvantage disappears in accounts of their dangerousness.

As political movements come to terms with their "terror of adolescence," the debates seem to coalesce around the suffering of those who are victims of violent crime. Fear of the crime that seems to be forever increasing is a powerful, personal and politically emotional tool. Ironically, fear of kids in Canada has been fuelled by two phenomena that are largely the result of business as usual. First, part of the problem has been the increased visibility of young people in public places. As industry has "rationalized" production by reducing employment costs, youth unemployment has risen, as high as 30 percent in some areas. More youth have increasingly more idle time, and the work that is available is poorly paid, bereft of benefits, and offers little in terms of meaningful apprenticeship. The typical employee at fast-food chains is the adolescent, the typical wage is at or just above minimum wage and the work is typically hard and sometimes dangerous. The typical benefits package is non-existent. Furthermore, the building of centralized shopping centres is not done with community solidarity in mind but is merely the result of profit considerations. That adolescents gather in such places is neither anathema to profit nor is it discouraged by private interests. And yet the presence of youth in places such as shopping malls fuels the panic that kids are loitering with the intent to commit a crime.

Second, most people gain their images and opinions about the nature and extent of crime through the media. In Canada much of our vicarious experience with youth crime is filtered through American television. American news, much of which teeters on the brink of fiction, is highly sensational, selective to time and place, and focuses primarily on the dangerous. I will argue later that such depictions are not based on reality but on the wants of a presumed audience. The news industry argues that its function is to present news accounts based on objective reality; more accurately, however, the industry constructs the news to appeal to the demands of a frightened audience and a political-economic system that casts blame.

What we are left with, then, is a gulf between reality and perception. The reality is that youth are mostly disenfranchised from the democratic process at all levels of governance, they are disadvantaged in the labour market and they have few services available to them, unlike their adult counterparts. When they do break the law, they victimize other youth who are like them. Furthermore, youth crime has not increased significantly, even though the prosecution of youth crime has. That reality stands in stark contrast to the collective perceptions that kids are out of control and more dangerous now than ever before, and that youth crime is expanding at an alarming rate.

How do we explain the existence of a belief system that moralizes about and condemns children in the face of contradictory evidence? Are we as a society so uncertain about our ability to raise children that we constantly question the culture of youth? Are we, in an adult-created and -based world, so unfamiliar with adolescent norms and social conventions that we are frightened by the unfamiliar? Or are there larger forces at work that construct, communicate and perpetuate a belief system that benefits those who have access to power and indicts and disadvantages those who live on the margins of society?

Moral Panics and Power

One of the important considerations in understanding moral panics as historical and socio-political phenomena is that they are not unique and evolutionary, but that they occur regularly and predictably throughout history. Much of the moral panic literature, common in critical criminological research of the late sixties and early seventies, has used historical analyses to study the phenomenon of putative crime waves and the origins of public panics about crime (Hall et al. 1978; Cohen 1980). The research concentrated on how atypical or rare events at historical junctures came to raise collective ire to the point where the public demanded law reform. In addition, the literature concentrated on how official and popular culture accounts of criminality were based on overgeneralized, inaccurate and stereotypical descriptions of criminals and their associations and how the public panics that resulted were mostly directed at working-class or marginalized people. Much of the research, in addition, concentrated on moral panics over youth crime, especially in relation to alienated, organized, gang-based delinquents.

Stanley Cohen's (1980) influential work developed the concept of moral panic to study and make sense of British society's alarm and attack on youth in the 1960s and early 1970s. His analysis of the construction of the "Mods and Rockers" illustrated how this political/linguistic device based on social stereotyping came to circumscribe youth misconduct. He also illustrated how the media, through their abilities to use evocative language and imagery, alerted the public to a potentially criminogenic youth, coined by Cohen as "folk devils." Cohen discovered that once the folk devil was identified by the mainstream media, the context for understanding youth crime was established. For example, the judiciary and the police overreacted to those identified as gang members and came to view the Mods and Rockers as a conspiratorial, well-organized force. Also significant, and important to this book, was the media's inordinate preoccupation with understanding the youth malefactor as a gang member and describing dangerous youth as well-organized conspiracies of defiance.

Equally important as his critical analysis of the media and political motives, however, was Cohen's specification of the connection between this particular moral panic and the social, political and economic atmosphere of 1960s England:

> The sixties began the confirmation of a new era in adult-youth relations. . . . What everyone had grimly prophesied had come true: high wages, the emergence of a commercial youth culture "pandering" to young people's needs . . . the permissive society, the coddling by the Welfare State. . . . The Mods and Rockers symbolized something far more important than what they actually did. They touched the delicate and ambivalent nerves through which post-war social change in Britain was experienced. No one wanted depression or austerity. . . . Resentment and jealousy were easily directed at the young because of their increased spending power and sexual freedom. (1980:192)

Hall et al. (1978) lent a more Marxist interpretation to the historical understanding of moral panics by suggesting that panics serve a decidedly elitist purpose. Their study of mugging in England in the 1970s suggested that the public and political alarm over street crime was created by the ruling elite in order to divert attention away from the crisis in British capitalism. As in other capitalist countries, increasing unemployment was being consciously used by business and government to re-establish general profit levels and to ostensibly fight inflation. In essence, high profits and high employment are anathema and inflationary. The British industrial state was in fiscal and social distress. To deflect attention away from the real causes of the fiscal crisis, according to Hall et al. (1978), authorities exaggerated the threat posed by street crime.

The work of Hall and his co-authors is particularly important and instructive in that it studies the connections between ideological production, the mass media and those in positions of power. Without this type of critical perspective, we are left with the presumption that the media acts alone, isolated from economy and politics, and that its mistaken mandate is the result of poor journalism and the requirement to compete in the supply and demand world of news. Just as I argue in this book, Hall et al. contend that one of the primary functions of the news is to give significance to events. In fact, the media both draw on and recreate consensus. This contention becomes apparent when we realize that the "media represent the primary, and often the only source of information about many important events and topics" (Hall et al. 1978:56). Furthermore, "the media define for the majority of the population what significant events are taking place, but, also, they offer powerful interpretations of how to understand these events" (Hall et al. 1978:57). And one of the important ways the news media maintain their power is by claiming journalistic objectivity as a priori. The ostensible task of the news media, then, is to sift fact from fiction and they do this by drawing on expert opinion. And as we will come to see later on in this book, expert opinion is an extremely common journalistic device, and such opinion is generally as wide and varied as it is plentiful.

The discourse of news is first and foremost ideological. That is, it is morality-laden language and the talk of privileged people. There is a structured relationship between the media and the ideas of the powerful sectors of the society. The creation, control and proliferation of journalistic discourse is constrained by definitions of right and wrong that are governed by powerful people, even if such people do not hold with such definitions. Capitalist power and its relations with politics are able to reproduce a morality that implies that certain people are better and more valuable than others on the basis of their place in the economic system. Such discourse serves to reproduce the socio-economic system that allows some to live in mansions and requires others to live on the streets, by organizing the way we think about crime and punishment in relation to poverty and wealth. Crime, as constructed and framed in public discourse, functions to legitimate and maintain class differences in all sectors of society. I will show later in this book that rarely do media accounts that equate crime with privation do so without discussing related issues of visible-minority-group membership and immigration, or single motherhood and the problems it poses to traditional family values.

Many of the panics that typified the 1960s and 1970s appear today in a similar form, if not content. In moral panics, public perceptions of the degree and form of violent crime are largely inaccurate and exaggerated (see Kappeler, Blumberg and Potter 1993; Painter 1993; Jenkins 1992). Although traditional research on moral panics dealt with "mainstream" deviances—drug use or witchcraft, for example—current research tends to concentrate more on what might be labelled shocking or lurid deviances: ritual abuse, serial murder, pedophilia and child abuse. One should not diminish the seriousness of these crimes, but it is important to note that, with the exception of child abuse, most of the phenomena under study are quite rare. And, as typified by past moral panics, rare occurrences nourish a general alarm over individual safety.

There is also a rapidly expanding body of literature that focuses on youth gangs, studying either the origins and activities of such gangs or public reactions to them. This rather orthodox, narrowly focused literature certainly helps legitimize the moral panic discourse. Ironically, little attention has been paid to the moral outrage that has greeted all youth, not just identifiable gang members, even though gang membership and race are often used to underscore the presumed violent and organized nature of youth crime. This is not to suggest that the moral panic surrounding youth crime is subtle or hidden. On the contrary, the attack on youth has been vocal, concerted and politicized, fostered by the portrayal of idiosyncratic examples of youth crime as typical. The existing public debates on youth crime, while largely uninformed, have the potency and the scientific legitimacy to direct public opinion and to effect social control policy that stigmatizes and controls those who are most disadvantaged and victimized.

I want to suggest that the primary effect of media and official accounts of youth crime is to decontextualize the acts for public consumption. Although the media may not directly control public opinion, they are certainly able to contain the nature of discourse by establishing parameters of discussion and by giving the appearance of consensus on public issues. The portraits of youth criminals that public crime accountants paint are largely of nihilistic, pathological criminals who act alone or as members of gangs, criminals who are devoid of a moral base. The decontextualization of youth crime, however, misses a fundamental consideration in understanding crime: most repeat young offenders and their families are victims of socio-economic conditions often beyond their control, and they are more than likely to be repeatedly victimized as clients of the systems of law, social welfare and education.

I contend that the powerful in society benefit from a particular "truth" about young offenders. The media images that we see push public discussion away from an understanding of youth crime that includes the effects of privation, disenfranchisement and marginalization and push it towards understandings based on individual morality or pathology. Those with corporate or state power are largely responsible for creating conditions that are detrimental to others. The attack on the deficit, which seems currently to drive many public policy initiatives, is detrimental to the least advantaged but advantageous to the already privileged. For example, state policy rarely attacks unfair or nonprogressive taxation, ostensibly for fear of alienating businesses and driving them elsewhere, especially in the context of free trade zones, such as that created by the North American Free Trade Agreement (NAFTA). The recourse then is to attack social-support programs, employment initiatives and education. The system of profit is absolved from responsibility for making the lives of others more precarious, and the result is social-support networks are destroyed. The law in its function as moral arbiter has a significant input into the way the public views the connections between crime and economy. The mandate of the law is to judge individual conduct primarily, although certainly not exclusively. In addition, the accounts of youth crime and justice fostered in the media focus almost exclusively on individual conduct and rarely on the criminogenic effect of the partnership between corporate capitalism and the state.

The Media and the Politics of Morality

Moral panics are characterized by their affiliations with politics, systems of information and various institutions of social control, including the legal system. The operation of a moral panic is both symbolic and practical, and functions within the confines of an orthodox state machinery that is closely tied to the mechanisms of production. Moral panics are constituted within a discourse that has a profound effect on public opinion; and media presentations of decontextualized events are a powerful way of legitimating punitive discourse.

In fact, moral panics may drive public policy and may also be created to justify political decisions already made.

The Symbolic Crusade

Most youth-focused crime panics urge others either to protect children or condemn them. Warnings that children are constantly in danger lead to lobbies against child abuse, child pornography, prostitution, pedophilia, serial killers, smoking and drunk driving. Alternately, those who believe that all children are potentially dangerous have lobbied for the reform of the Young Offenders Act, implementation of dangerous offender legislation and increased use of custodial dispositions for young offenders. Pessimism about and distrust of children is apparent in many news articles that suggest blatantly that children are not to be trusted or taken lightly. Our ambivalence between protecting and condemning children is embodied in our cultural approach to child rearing, which advocates both affection/protection and physical punishment. Further, it is ironic that we tend to punish those who are both most dear to us, our children (in the form of family discipline), and those who are farthest removed from us, the hardened criminals (in penal institutions).

The growing focus on criminogenic children not only implies that the powerful are better, but it also diverts public debate away from the political actions of the powerful that create social stresses for the less powerful (unemployment, welfare-state cuts, dangerous work environments, poorly paid and part-time labour). In addition, child-focused panics seem to set the limits of social tolerance and seek to change the moral and legal environment to reflect those limits. While harm to children is the threshold of tolerance, child-centred symbolic lobbies reflect the belief that children are also unpredictable and volatile as a subculture. The attendant rhetoric invokes images of gangs, and connections between nihilistic behaviour and music and dress (grunge, as a typical example). The youth subculture is, in general, portrayed as aimless and calculating. The anti-youth lobby is a potent symbolic mechanism for framing youth crime—and ultimately all conduct—in ambivalent yet moralistic terms.

The Interdependence of Panics

Moral panics emerge in clusters and tend to foster one another. The current movements in Canada directed at gun control, the drug trade, gang violence, car theft and dangerous offenders all make reference to youth involvement. Highly sensational incidents are interpreted as part of an overall social menace, and subsequent events are viewed within this gestalt of fear and framed in fear-provoking language. The success of one panic lends credibility to another, and the result is a generalized lobby for increased social control at all levels. For example, when issues of youth crime and violence predominate on the airwaves, there are usually concurrent discussions of teen sexuality, youth prostitution and unwed motherhood. Issues of youth exploitation and disadvantage become linked by temporal association to issues of youth menace, resulting in a generalized "problem of youth." The lumping together of adolescent issues transforms a problem that originates with the structure of society into one that appears to originate with youth themselves. The state and the adult world are absolved from responsibility for the exploitation of children and are removed from the attendant social categories that delinquent children represent.

The Role of the Mass Media

The Canadian newspaper and television industries seem to be continually moving towards monopolization by a few major media corporations. In effect, there is currently very little competition for the moral attention of Canadians. In fact, at the time of writing this book, Conrad Black, who owns forty or more newspapers around the world, purchased the four major daily newspapers in the province of Saskatchewan and, in typical corporate rationalization, the company immediately laid off one-quarter of the newspaper employees in the province. The newspaper industry's passion for profit also results in the production of sensationalist and often uncontested news accounts that appear fictitious and largely removed from the social and economic context in which they occur but are, more likely than not, highly marketable. The primary functions of media portraits of crime include: (1) the creation of a world of insiders and outsiders, and acceptability and unacceptability, in order to facilitate public demand and consumption; (2) the connecting of images of deviance and crime with social characteristics; and (3) the decontextualization of crime in anecdotal evidence that is presented as omnipresent, noncomplex truth.

The Interdependence of Institutions

Moral crusades are often typified by the collaboration of various institutions of social control. Institutions such as medicine, education, social welfare, religion and government are all involved in the work of understanding and controlling youth crime. It is not surprising, then, that public accounts of youth crimes or of a general youth crime epidemic draw on experts from these institutions to lend credibility to their claims and persuade audiences that the concern for growing youth crime is legitimate and widespread. And politicians are quick to adopt a punitive stance towards youth, especially on behalf of conservative business and community leaders. As we will see, the interdependent and multi-institutional nature of moral panics is an important focus for the critical researcher in uncovering the claims to moral legitimacy made in public discourse, and in revealing the actors who benefit from such claims.

Conclusion

In this book I seek to place the moral panic against youth in an explanatory framework. The area of youth crime and justice has been inundated with critical and consensus theories that have attempted to understand why youths choose to break the law or how societies are responsible for creating the conditions under which young people will end up at odds with society. The orientation of this book is both critical and social constructionist. The critical position stems from debates on the concept of the moral panic in the late 1960s and early 1970s. The corpus of this work attempted to unpack the hidden agenda behind the creation of a mythology of delinquency. In this book I accept the challenge of that mythology as well. I discuss the advantages that accrue to the influential players in this public debate; how they construct and produce images of deviance that absolve them from responsibility for social conditions and indict others who are less powerful; and how constructed images of good and evil infiltrate the public consciousness to the degree that young people are excluded from the common good. This book, then, is essentially a study of ideology—a collective belief system that constricts the way we see the world, especially with respect to issues of good and evil. Ultimately, such a belief system ties good and evil to socio-economics.

The social-constructionist approach presumes that knowledge (social and "natural" facts) is largely created, most often for a political purpose. The primary assumptions are that even the most "objective" knowledge is relative to time and place, and that experts who are charged with understanding criminality are powerful constructors of portraits of crime. Discourse, knowledge and power are inextricably connected in this paradigm, which awakens us to the need to deconstruct official and public opinions.

Overall, the sociological sensitivity to young offenders is important in unpacking the forces that would blame children for social ills and at the same time denounce anyone who would endanger children. I believe that this contradictory and unnerving posture towards Canada's youth can only be understood within a political-economic framework that poses the following question: If children are our most cherished resource, why then do we denounce and fear adolescence and ultimately discard children for political and moral ends?

Chapter 2

Actors in the Theatre of Crime

The theatrical depiction of public panics in this book is a deliberate metaphor intended to emphasize the fictional and constructed nature of events presumed to be factual, and to illustrate that the consumer or reader is compelled or at least invited to empathize with the victim or the hero who solves a problem.

As with most issues involving public opinion, the majority of players in the drama benefit and may be distinguished by their degree of self-interest and volition. These beneficiaries are the direct and indirect authors of the fiction. In general, beneficiaries gain economic, political, cultural or moral advantage from portraits that are intended to distance the creators from the protagonists. In the context of the current panic over youth crime, the beneficiaries are myriad but interrelated and include everyone but the victim and the folk devil.

The Press

If we accept for the moment Marshall McLuhan's aphorism that "the medium is the message," then we also can accept his contention that "the owners of media always endeavour to give the public what it wants, because they sense that their power is in the *medium* and not in the *message* or the program" (1964:193). This suggests several things: that media producers give us what they think we want to hear and not necessarily the facts; that the television, radio and print media are so ambient that they are "staples or natural resources, exactly as are coal and cotton and oil"; and that "our human senses, of which all media are extensions, . . . configure the awareness and experience of each one of us" (McLuhan 1964:35). The media have the power to construct slanted or fictional accounts of real-life incidents by decontextualizing and simplifying the news. The resulting binary depictions are presented as unambiguous accounts of good and evil, offering us, at best, supposedly what we want to hear and, at worst, all we are capable of understanding.

Kellner (1995) has warned us that as we live in a media and consumer society, we run the risk of passively accepting what we see and read without questioning the content or the moral message. He argues that the media is the consummate ideological tool.

> Radio, television, film and the other products of media culture provide materials out of which we forge our very identities, our sense of selfhood; our notion of what it means to be male or female; our sense of class, of ethnicity and race, of nationality, of sexuality, of "us" and

"them." Media images help shape our view of the world and our deepest values: what we consider good or bad, positive or negative, moral or evil. Media stories provide the symbols, myths and resources through which we constitute a common culture and through the appropriation of which we insert ourselves into this culture. Media spectacles demonstrate who has power and who is powerless, who is allowed to exercise force and violence and who is not. They dramatize and legitimate the power of the forces that be and show the powerless that they must stay in their places or be destroyed. (1995:5)

Ultimately, the media provides the discourse used to understand things that happen in the real world. Neil Postman has argued that television is the modern medium that establishes the tools for viewing, reading and understanding:

We have reached, I believe, a critical mass in that electronic media have decisively and irreversibly changed the character of our symbolic environment. We are now a culture whose information, ideas and epistemology are given form by television, not by the printed word. To be sure, there are still readers and there are many books published but the uses of print and reading are not the same as they once were; not even in schools, the last institutions where print was thought to be invincible. They delude themselves who believe that television and print coexist, for coexistence implies parity. There is no parity here. Print is now merely a residual epistemology, and it will remain so, aided to some extent by the computer, and newspapers and magazines that are made to look like television screens. (1985:28)

The advent of television marks a watershed in human history when we no longer needed to pay attention for lengthy periods of time. Television made it possible to ingest images without having to spend time doing so. The impact of our shortened attention span is that we are unreceptive to contextualized accounts. For example, when we read oversized, alarmist headlines or see pictures in magazines of kids wielding guns, these images often satiate our interest. Postman and others have argued that television has done this to us, that it has created a discourse of abbreviated images and messages from which we cannot escape. It would be impossible, for example, to listen to hours-long political speeches today: in the past, public forum political debates were grand social events and the speakers held the audience's attention for hours. The last vestige of this in the Canadian political arena existed during the Diefenbaker/Pearson era in Canada and during the Kennedy era in America when oratory and sustained accounts were still the norm. These were probably the last professional orators; they gave way to the electronic media era and the shortened public attention span.

I part company with authors like Postman and McLuhan. Although I agree that television circumscribes public discourse in the modern world, other types of media have adjusted to the visual discourse and become like a kind of typographic television. Magazines, newspapers and the internet use television techniques to sell their messages. The fundamental consideration in the age of television is that what we see and read must entertain. This has profound implications for the news media; its primary function, in competition for the attention of the viewing public, is to use journalistic "facts" in an entertaining way. And this is what we see in modern news media accounts, some of which I analyze in this book. Because of the highly profitable nature of "the news," a vast and expanding body of discursive techniques have arisen, the most recent being the internet, which permits access to international images and accounts in seconds. Much like the truncated portraits typical of television, internet news sources are necessarily brief, often accompanied by photographs and often unabashedly biased. But we need look no farther than the grocery store check-out stand or magazine rack to see that the print medium has proliferated despite the ubiquity of television. The "new typography" is more photography than print, as this medium attempts to emulate television. Even within television itself, intense competition for the public's attention creates various forms of docu-dramas, daytime talk shows that purport to deal with real-life issues, "true crime" shows in which the camera follows law enforcement officials, actual courtroom eavesdropping and the ultimate technique exemplified by the O.J. Simpson phenomena, the real-life soap opera.

Despite this profusion of discursive vehicles, my focus here is on newspapers and news magazines, principally because these two media have not diminished but have changed in form and content to compete in the electronic era. The tabloid newspaper, typical of the Sun chain, is an attempt to make the newspaper easier to handle on the bus, in the car or while standing on the street corner, all situations that allow only brief periods of time to ingest the news. Magazines of all stripes, including news magazines, proliferate in public places—including the waiting rooms of doctors, dentists, mechanics, hairdressers and lawyers, to name a few. Although these may appear to be banal examples of access to news discourse, I contend that the accounts found within these magazines reach a wide audience; however, they are viewed in a very cursory way, the time span of reading is short and the visual images are their most influential components. Although I have no hard evidence regarding the degree of public exposure, I was recently struck by an experience that indicated to me the power of the magazine, even in relation to television. I entered a waiting room in a large automobile repair chain and sat among ten or eleven patrons waiting for their automobiles. A television was hanging in the corner of the room and a daytime soap was on. What interested me was that all of the individuals in the room were reading magazines and newspapers, and only rarely glancing up at the images on the screen. This indicates, if only in an anecdotal way, the allure of the magazine and the newspaper, especially when time is limited.

What I am suggesting is that the print media are still profoundly influential, and the photographs and headlines are what the cursory reader sees and likely remembers most. The short attention span of the modern reader is vulnerable to images that are necessarily simplistic and decontextualized. A television-based discourse provides "news" accounts of crime that can only be taken and understood out of context, and thus crime becomes fiction.

The Epistemological Power of the News Media

The media responds to the pressure of supply and demand in producing news for mass consumption. By creating sensationalist accounts of real-life incidents, supposedly to appeal to the prurient desires in most readers and viewers, the media has exceptional political and ideological power; they create a world of us and them, of insiders and outsiders. In so doing, the media embed stereotypical images of deviants and menaces in our collective psyches that inform us as we form opinions about crime and punishment.

The formative power of the media is more complex than I have stated. That the media has epistemological influence has been well voiced over decades (McLuhan 1964; Iyengar and Kinder 1987; Kellner 1995), but this argument stands in contradiction to those made by media economists who contend that the media respond in a supply-and-demand manner to the wishes of the consumer. This supply-and-demand position is somewhat banal in its implication that people democratically control what they see and how they understand what they see. Although I do not vehemently deny this position, I feel strongly that the panics and hatred that modern society has formed regarding young people are, at least in part, the results of constructed, controlled and decontextualized images of kids.

The fears and concerns that generated my writing of this book are that media depictions of young criminals as the new folk devils are fraught with biased images of gender, class, race and ethnicity. My analysis of the print media is based on the position that the public's common-sense understandings of young criminals originate with fictionalized, distorted, stereotypical accounts of young offenders and their socio-economic affiliations. Furthermore, those who present these partial images have a two-dimensional vested interest, at once economic and ideological.

One of the fundamental tenets of a free press is that reporters are not constrained by any outside force to present the news in a particular way. Rather, the news reporter takes an implicit oath to report the facts objectively and without bias. Marshall McLuhan, however, first awakened us to the likelihood that the message we receive is dependent on the medium and on those in positions of ownership. His admonition that the "medium is the message" (1964) was a forewarning that our ideas and opinions are largely influenced by self-interested, biased mediators of the news. The news media especially shapes the way we think about things that are foreign and frightening to us. Despite the fact that violent youth crime is a statistical rarity and that the victims are primarily other youth of the same social categories, the general populace perceives modern youth as increasingly violent and dangerous.

But three other features of the news media warrant discussion. First, the Canadian newspaper industry is increasingly becoming monopolized by a few major media corporations. In effect, there is very little competition for the moral attention of Canadians (cf. Hackett 1991:91–92; *Maclean's,* November 11, 1996). Second, like most corporate entities, the "press"—at least at the decision-making/editorial level—is comprised of reporters, editors, producers, presenters and executive officers who are primarily white and male and privileged— very much unlike the people who are the targets of their accounts. Third, the newspaper industry is a highly competitive industry and is increasingly in competition with American news organizations for the public's attention. The news media are also increasingly in competition with para-factual news accounts based on real-life events that are presented in a decontextualized, fictional style (for example, "Cops" and "Hard Copy"). Talk shows help erase the distinction between fact and fiction by profiling individual cases as typical of larger social phenomena. The entertainment industry has invaded the news arena and obliterated the distinction between objectivity and subjectivity. One of the singular characteristics of late twentieth-century news reporting is that news is now, more than ever, a commodity that must be desirable and titillating if it is to sell.

The media do not just sell news, however, they sell audiences and programming to advertisers. As Hackett (1991) argues, advertisers are interested in two kinds of audiences: the affluent and the mass audience. Newspapers and news magazines are prepared to pay more to reach affluent audiences because of the high purchasing power of these audiences. Most importantly, however, "Affluent readers are more likely to be politically conservative, and they have a disproportionate 'vote' in determining the type and the political orientations of the media that survive" (Hackett 1991:69). In addition, as the media becomes more monopolized, more concentrated and less competitive, the number of alternative voices and opinions diminishes, especially with respect to important political and social issues. This narrowing of opinion may not necessarily reflect consumer demand in general but rather the demands of particular consumers— advertisers and well-heeled audiences who need and prefer a particular world view and a particular take on social issues. This elitist world view is narrowly moral and necessarily alarmist.

The Consumer

The media's efforts to accentuate certain types of news is based on the presumption that what the public fears, the public will read. Like fictional television, the task of the news media is to simplify the world into binary opposites: good and evil, safe and frightening and, most importantly, us and them. For reasons of marketing and competition, the media simplify the world for public consumption. The "mythical accounts" they present become an omnipresent truth that, through the democratic process, drives public policy. The obvious case in point is the current law reform surrounding the Young Offenders Act that is being struck to create a harsher youth justice system despite evidence that youth crime is not epidemic (Schissel 1993).

The civil libertarian's response to biased news accounts is simply to "let the buyer beware." The suggestion is that if people do not like watching, reading or listening to partisan accounts of crime and deviance, then they have the freedom not to. Unfortunately, television is so much a part of ambient culture that the resolve not to listen is rarely possible; school-aged children spend more time with the television than they do with their parents. More importantly, as television continues to replace all other forms of media in the creation and transportation of news, the embracing nature of its influence becomes more alarming. The intrusive nature of television does not allow people to simply turn it off or tune out:

> Television has achieved the status of meta-medium—an instrument that directs not only our knowledge of the world, but our knowledge of ways of knowing as well . . . television has achieved the status of "myth," as Roland Barthes uses the word. He means by myth a way of understanding the world that is not problematic, that we are not fully conscious of, that seems, in a word, natural. A myth is a way of thinking so deeply embedded in our consciousness that it is invisible. This is the way of television. . . . Television has become . . . the background radiation of the social and intellectual universe, the all-but-impercep-tible residue of the electronic big bang of a century past, so familiar and so thoroughly integrated with American culture that we no longer hear its faint hissing in the background or see the flickering gray light. This, in turn, means that its epistemology goes largely unnoticed. And the peek-a-boo world it has constructed around us no longer seems even strange. (Postman 1985:78–79)

I disagree, however, with the contention that "[w]e are now a culture whose information, ideas and epistemology are given form by television, not by the printed word" (Postman 1985:28). I argue that the print medium, in its need to appeal to the widest possible audience, has in fact adapted to the television world by becoming more like television in its fictional content and in its presentation of decontextualized, brief and episodic accounts. And, this pseudo-fact-based appeal to large audiences is what I believe is at the heart of accounts of youth crime and justice in Canada's print medium. Further, given the increasingly monopolistic trend in the Canadian newspaper and magazine industries, no longer can newspapers and magazines continue to appeal to a specific reading audience. The point is that the news media, now more than ever, appeal to the prurient interests of the reading public (or, more correctly, watching public), and the result is that the industry not only reacts to what the public wants, but also proactively creates and directs the public appetite. A cursory look at a supermarket check-out newsstand provides clear evidence that the world of fact and fiction is becoming more and more confused and fused, and that the images are less verbal and more pictorial than in the past.

One of the ways television has monopolized the attention of the public is by presenting very perfunctory versions of a large number of topics in a short period of time. To do this effectively, the medium uses pictorial images to bombard the viewers senses with unconnected impressions. These impressions are of events that "do not arise out of historical conditions but rather explode from the heavens in a series of disasters that suggest a permanent state of crisis" (Postman 1988:80). Increasingly, the different print media use visual images in disconnected contexts to create a television effect. As I will illustrate later, magazines especially use stereotypical images to confront our emotions around fear and security. These visual images are used by the newspaper industry as well, which also employs shocking headlines.

The audience for these theatrics comprises unwilling consumers. I do not mean to suggest that people do not have volition, I mean that news accounts that are presented in simplistic and consumable packages are so pervasive and available that the busy modern consumer cannot help but be affected, if only subliminally. The news media, both factual and para-factual, have a great deal of influence on the modern mind, not necessarily because the people involved in the news are evil or manipulative, but rather because the market structure of the media industry dictates that the primary function of news reporting is that people pay attention, which is the ultimate objective of advertising. Because the consumer, and not journalistic fidelity, is the focus of the news report, the mythical accounts of crime that pervade the news present a rather unmanageable world. The consumer is left with a sense of disjointedness and with a view of the world as one in which human community does not work and violence and personal trauma are everpresent. The news industry's presentation of a nihilistic society is no accident. Such presentations are constructed to sell and, importantly, "they generate meaning as well as profit" (Hackett 1991:51). The most insidious result of this manipulation is that the news business acts as a "filter, gatekeeper, or agenda setter" (Hackett 1991:52) that provides powerful citizens with a mechanism to direct public opinion. This is exactly what has happened to the mythology of youth crime in Canada.

Governments

The control of crime is essentially a political act; it involves the domination of wealthy men over poor men, of men over women, of politically powerful racial groups over marginalized racial minorities, and of enfranchised adults over children. If we understand this, it is not difficult to see how issues of crime and punishment become politicized. As public fears about street crime and personal safety are manipulated—while the dangers of corporate and organizational crime are diminished—the central role of public opinion in the democratic process comes to the fore. Political platforms are almost without exception based on issues of crime and punishment. In the last two decades of the millennium, right-wing political movements have been fraught with arguments and images of a growing criminal underclass that increasingly preys on ordinary citizens. This fear and loathing is a natural playground for politicians. It is basic, cataclysmic and demands severe and immediate intervention. Although some politicians understand that panics are exaggerated—e.g., Liberal Minister Alan Rock's admission that the Young Offenders Act is not responsible for youth crime and that Canada is not suffering an epidemic of crimes by youth—they often choose to engage in moral panic debates to appeal to the electorate. Of course, no savvy and/or moral politician would oppose anything that protects the vulnerability of ordinary citizens. Unfortunately, the perception and the reality are often disconnected. It appears that those in power and those who administer this power pick an easy target, and these targets are the disaffiliated and the disenfranchised. Government is essentially about taking sides.

It is also important to understand that governments have the power and ability to contribute facts to the mythmaking mechanism. The Foucauldian perspective later outlined in Chapter 6 addresses how knowledge brokers, especially those who have access to specialized information, can create and control a "reality." Government data is a powerful source of information that is often used in attempts to understand antisocial behaviour. Government documents have greater legitimacy because they are (1) based on empirically gained information (the census and government surveys), (2) in the public domain (but only in an ideal sense, in that they are difficult to access, especially for the layperson), (3) mystical unless the viewer understands quantitative social research methods, (4) necessarily decontextualized and, consequently, (5) often mediated by experts (it is at this point that expertise becomes impression management).

Many news reports that focus on youth crime invoke government-based information as infallible. Government crime statistics provide a sense of how much crime is occurring and how rates have changed over time. The problem is that statistics are based on police or court records and not on actual crimes committed; they are open to interpretation and offer no explanation or context for things that happen. As a result, crime rates are an indication of the workings of the justice system rather than the nature of criminality. They are also often an indication of how crime is defined and categorized. Youth crime statistics often group many types of crimes together. The moral panic surrounding youth has used official total crime rates to argue that youth crime is epidemic. The interpretable reality, however, is that much of current youth crime is based on violations of the Young Offenders Act by rather harmless acts of vandalism and schoolyard antagonism. To group these offenses with offenses that create fear and panic is to severely exaggerate and distort the reality of youth misconduct. Official crime rates are often an indication of the political climate at any point in time. A large body of current research has argued that official crime and imprisonment rates fluctuate primarily as a result of changes in socio-economic and political conditions and not as a result of increases in crimes committed or in policing and incarceration (Schissel 1992; Cantor and Land 1985). Simply put, government policy, not criminals, creates crime rates.

The Policers

Although the police are the front-line protectors of the society, they also have a good deal of influence and discretion in producing images of criminality. In fairness to the police, they often respond to public and political demands and, to this end, are merely fulfilling the democratic promise to protect. Their democratic mandate is not only to police reactively but to proactively intervene before crimes occur. The concept of proactive intervention, or crime prevention, is part of the current vernacular of community justice and social health and is considered by policymakers as a more effective and less expensive method of securing a safe society. But in their struggle to discharge the community policing mandate, the police often take it upon themselves to focus on ostensibly criminogenic neighbourhoods, generally in the inner city where police are more numerous, visible and assertive. This activity also fulfils a second function for the police: their existence, popularity and growth is based on increasing the scope and intensity of law enforcement in marginalized neighbourhoods. In an ironic sense, real crime prevention is anathema to popular and expanding police forces.

In discussing the role of the police in moral panics, it is difficult to place blame or even responsibility. The police have a crime-control mandate that is concordant with orthodox law-and-order justice policies, but the police are not trained to be peace officers. They are, as a consequence, constrained politically and professionally to act swiftly and dramatically. Part of this has to do with both preservation of the self and preservation of the reputation of the police force. The police, as front-line workers, have vast credibility in the eyes of the public. Unfortunately, when they panic, their actions echo quickly, and their consequent and continual lack of reflexivity and self-analysis is potentially harmful for targets of public panics. Furthermore, it may be police bureaucrats and not front-line officers who are most responsible for fomenting panic. Police management is not only responsible for helping to set and implement the crime-control mandate—in lieu of the peace officer mandate—but they also selectively present crime accounts to public officials and the media by choosing to release specific sorts of information.

Moralizing Groups

Howard Becker (1963) coined the term *moral entrepreneur* to refer to individuals who took a proactive role in defining and controlling deviant behaviour. The moral entrepreneur is someone who has a vested interest in seeing the moral movement come to fruition; is a moral crusader who believes that an identifiable segment of the population is acting immorally; and has the influence, credibility and power to put his or her beliefs into the public arena. For Becker (1963), moral entrepreneurs were "rule creators" who operate from a self-righteous, elitist world view and/or "rule enforcers" who operate from a more pragmatic, "job well done" world view but often share the same value system as a rule creator.

At the time of Becker's work, it was clear that there were many historical examples of moral entrepreneurs who had been able to affect public policy. In Canada, for example, the influences of Mackenzie King and Emily Murphy on Canadian drug legislation (cf. Comack 1991; Green 1986) are noteworthy. In the United States, the influence of Harry Anslinger, the head of the Federal Bureau of Narcotics, in the creation of the Marijuana Tax Act is typical of the 1930–1960 era in North America (cf. Becker 1963). These individuals with political power were able almost singlehandedly to initiate public policy on the basis of assumed dangerous groups or "folk devils." In both jurisdictions, the folk devils were ethnic minorities who were politically and democratically marginalized: Chinese immigrants in Canada and Mexican immigrants in the United States.

Modern-day moral movements, unlike those in the past, are less directed by individuals and more directed by political/doctrinal groups that have a strong, vested economic interest in creating a stricter, more punitive and less forgiving society. Many moral entrepreneurial groups are closely connected to orthodox political or religious groups. Although public leaders spearhead these groups— I refer to political leaders such as Preston Manning and the Reform Party in Canada, and Newt Gingrich and the Republican right in the United States—it is unlikely that these individuals have personal influence. Rather, they tap into an existent public fervour for their own political credibility and exacerbate the emotional level of the debates.

When looking at reform groups, a central question seems to be whether such groups hold more sophisticated or at least more grounded understandings of social phenomena than do the media or political leaders. I would suggest that this probably is the case; yet when media or political accounts of crime are infused with blame and danger, reform groups are intensely vulnerable to impression management. As Cohen (1980) argues, there must be a potential or a volatility towards overreaction and panic among the public. Why such groups tend to err on the side of right-wing, punitive politics, however, is a fundamental question that has to do with understanding the forces that create and control pubic discourse.

The Victim

In the criminal justice system the victim is often forgotten when it comes time to decide on guilt or innocence, and especially in decisions regarding punishment. Victim welfare is rarely involved in judicial decisions. However, when public panics arise over supposed increases in crime, the victim does become the focus of concern. (Many of the media representations discussed in Chapter 4 are presented from the point of view of the victim's experience.) Punishment-based political lobbies argue that they are protecting the innocent victim when they advocate harsher law-and-order policies. And the victim's experience is a powerful political tool, because we all, at one time or another, visualize being victims of crime. It is relatively easy, therefore, for political persuaders to convince us to empathize with the plight of victims.

Victimization is used as a discursive mechanism in two ways. First, textual and pictorial depictions of victims' experiences are intended to evoke very primal and passionate responses to crime and our own and others' potential victimization. The vicarious victim's experience frames our understanding of the criminal event and creates empathy not only for the victim but also for advocates of law and order. Second, explanations for youth deviance are made in the context of family and cultural victimization, and the insinuations include mother-centred and lower-class families as potentially predatory on their children.

We are left, then, with these dual accounts of victimization, which establish that there is a need for panic and that innocent children are the victims of an uncaring, dangerous and poor class. Of course, victimization is a real problem that impacts on people's lives. Crime demands real solutions. This contention is difficult to refute or ignore. However, the concept of victimization can also be used as a volatile and powerful discursive tool to evoke collective passions and feed law-and-order politics.

What is missing, then, from these essentially popular cultural depictions of crime is a sense of larger victimization at the structural level—its context. Ordinary depictions of crime are usually decontextualized and constituted in discourse that is at once believable, instructive and policy-forming. There is thus a need to unpack the language of labelling, to identify the political and economic forces that drive the discourse and to analyze the political and economic advantages that accrue to the privileged from the denigration of marginalized and relatively powerless people.

Most importantly from a social justice point of view, crime panics and harsh law-and-order programs ignore a fundamental consideration in understanding crime: most repeat young offenders and their families are victims of *privation*. They have more than likely been repeatedly victimized by the systems of law, social welfare and education. These claims are harshly rejected by conservative political movements, which argue that people break the law for individualistic reasons and that, in a free society, people have the freedom to choose between

29

right and wrong. This compelling and simplistic libertarian position is difficult to refute in a democratic society. I will show in Chapter 5, however, that for understanding repeat young offenders, knowing the background of victimization and privation is more compelling and profound than the freedom-of-choice argument.

The Expert

Language and knowledge are social constructions and have political power. They can define and explain "reality" and tell the "truth." People who foster and use moral panics have a vested interest in making their truth claims as valid and legitimate as possible. Here the expert comes into play. These experts— academics, doctors, pollsters, police and court officials—have access to a specialized knowledge and language that is both mystical and impressive. The credibility of many media and political accounts of crime is based on the "expert" testimony of relatively privileged people; it is important to realize that professional testifiers are rarely drawn from the socio-economic strata occupied by stereotypical street criminals. We thus discredit common knowledge and folk wisdom and rely on the opinions of the educated. This is changing somewhat with the advent of community-based models of justice such as Aboriginal healing circles that rely on the collective wisdom and advice of people from all socio-economic backgrounds.

It is important to note that professional knowledge is often uncertain and contradictory regarding the nature of crime and the use of punishment. That is, following Foucault, knowledge is essentially created and not discovered, and knowledge in even the most "hard" sciences (such as the medical and physical sciences) changes depending on its political and historical context. As I will illustrate in Chapter 4, representations of youth crime often draw on selected opinions that are not necessarily shared by the majority in the scientific community. The credibility of the expert's statement therefore results from the credentials of the author of the opinion and not from the credibility of the account.

The Folk Devil

Finally we come to the focus of public panic. Cohen (1980) used the term *folk devil* to refer to those who were identified as threats to the moral and physical well-being of society. Importantly, the folk devil is identified by association with a particular, visible social category. Folk devils are inherently deviant and are presumed to be self-seeking, out of control and in danger of undermining the stability of society. Folk devils are constructed in the context of moral panic and are imbued with stereotypical characteristics that set them apart from normal, law-abiding society, making it easy for average citizens to become embroiled in the alarm over crime and to call for harsh justice. Most media depictions of crime, whether factual and fictional, are about people unlike us—the street person, the drug trafficker, the violent and the amoral. However, in the case of youth crime, and indeed adult crime as well, this stereotype is largely inaccurate. In fact, most youth commit crimes at one time or another and their crimes are transitory and involve very little harm (Snyder and Sickmund 1995; Schissel 1993). I contend, however, that the creation of the folk devil as a type of "resident alien" is the primary reason why punishment-based lobbies are so successful. It is difficult to punish people like us or our children, but much easier to punish those we do not understand or with whom we do not empathize. The creation of folk devils is a kind of xenophobia.

Essentially, then, this book is about the politics of hatred and the politics of fear. Hatred and fear are political emotions that people in positions of political and economic power use to garner public opinion. Fear and hatred are staples of popular culture and populist politics, and they are marked by their ambient and furtive nature. They exist as an unquestioned part of our ideology and discourse. Hatred is fundamental to news accounts, and fear is what sells them.

In *The Politics of Everyday Fear,* Massumi (1993) argues that our social spaces have been saturated by fear, and that fear is a basis for collective social experience. I would add that fear and hatred also contribute to a collective understanding of issues of right and wrong, which, incidentally, have little to do with a universal or inherent morality. Most importantly, fear and hatred are not abstractions and not the result of power in a theoretical form, but they result from the actual imposition of moral will by some over others. This imposition of will flourishes in public discourse, in which some speakers are more educated and consequently more influential than others.

The politics of fear and hatred are the mechanisms through which we attach moral valuations to social categories. If we hate and fear someone, then they must be bad. The xenophobia collectively felt towards young people, when unpacked, reveals an ideological orientation that associates immorality with marginal social groups, which are identifiable by race, class and gender. The politics of fear and hatred is, thus, in its basic form, the politics of stratification.

Chapter 3

Media Discourse and the Deconstruction of Crime Myths

Media representations of youth crime illustrate the power of decontextualized accounts and the ability of the media to represent the unusual as usual. These essentially ideological portraits of crime and criminals use selected, extraordinary crimes as evidence for a general crime wave and receive little or no public censure. When analyzing crime accounts, notice the initial written and visual messages that appear. The first few paragraphs and the prominent pictures are often television-like, perfunctory and cryptic. Postman argues that the

> news of the day is a figment of our technological imagination. It is quite precisely a media event. We attend to fragments of events from all over the world because we have multiple media whose forms are well suited to fragmented conversation. (1985:8)

That the medium dictates the message is worth repeating here because it raises the fundamental crisis confronted by the print medium: the ability of television to capture viewers' attention. Television, in fact, sets the standards for viewer/reader likes and dislikes. Postman reiterates the importance of television in framing the modern ethic:

> [T]he most significant American cultural fact of the second half of the twentieth century: the decline of the Age of Typography and the ascendancy of the Age of Television. This change-over has dramatically and irreversibly shifted the content and meaning of public discourse, since two media so vastly different cannot accommodate the same ideas. As the influence of the print wanes, the content of politics, religion, education, and anything else that comprises public business must change and be recast in terms that are most suitable to television. (1985:8)

If attention to the written word is limited, as has been suggested for TV-generation consumers (Postman 1994), the things encountered first in newspaper and magazine articles are what imprint on the minds of the cursory reader. When this television-like discourse (both visual and lingual) is studied carefully and critically, it becomes obvious that its messages are subtle, politically palatable, ideologically directed and very damaging to the image of youth. The depictions are not all the same, however, and can be categorized according to how they manage and manipulate the message. Nonetheless, the message is the same, and it is simple: youth crime is endemic, it is unpredictable but character-istic of a certain kind of youth and it requires dramatic and stern intervention. The remainder of this chapter illustrates the strategies the news media employ to create a particular, partial view of youth crime that is deliberately biased against all youth, but most specifically against youths who occupy particular socio-economic positions. The strategy for choosing newspaper and news magazine articles was based on a comprehensive survey of the Canadian print news media since 1988. The articles I chose present views of youth crime that are unusually slanted and non-objective. Amazingly, I encountered very few even-handed, objective accounts of youth crime in news articles from this time period. Although the articles for this book were not selected at random, they are representative of the type of account most often found in the news media. Admittedly, the magazine articles are primarily from *Maclean's, Alberta Report* and *Western Report* and might thus present a Western bias. However, these are political magazines whose focus is often crime and law, and they are the magazines that seem most often to speak to these issues.

Youth Crime and the Morality Play

The first category of stories includes depictions of unusual youth crimes that appeal to people's sense of despair by concentrating on the potentiality and horror of violent behaviour and bystander apathy. The accounts present youth crime as inexplicable and ultimately unthinkable. This type of depiction provides a reverse morality play that appeals to our sense of righteousness and our fear of an amoral world. Most importantly, such accounts provide constant and pervasive messages about the connections between morality and social position and, though they may attempt to be even-handed and objective, they lapse into social censure.

Such a media account involves the case of James Bulger, a two-year-old British child who was abducted by two boys under the age of thirteen in a Liverpool shopping centre, dragged away along a railway track and beaten to death. This incident happened in plain view of passers-by, who failed to help, for reasons speculated on at great length by the media.

This case is noteworthy in part for the horrific nature of the crime and the fact that the perpetrators were so young, but it is most noteworthy because it evolved into a morality play. As Bradley (1994:12) argues, "This rarest of murders has been transformed into a symbol of everything that is wrong with Britain today." The search for a rational explanation for the murders that predominated the initial media focus was replaced by a protracted campaign to understand this crime as the result of the worst side of the human condition. The argument that evil incarnate is part of human nature seeks to forewarn us that all citizens have the potential to become like the murderers of James Bulger. If ten-year-olds, who in our estimation are too young to have had the chance to become corrupted, are capable of this behaviour, then so are we all.

The class-based nature of this account became evident, however, when newspapers such as the *London Sun* and the *Evening Standard* began speculating about the potential of certain kinds of families to persist outside of civilized society. It is at this point that state institutions (including the justice system and social services), conservative politicians and investigative reporters engaged in a new type of class-oriented rhetoric surrounding the competency of parents in raising moral children. All three of these sources of opinion began to discuss the parents of the accused as part of a flawed underclass with typically pejorative attributes such as single motherhood and broken homes. The discourse centred on classic cases of abuse and neglect that were deemed to be the result of privation; by extension, all children living in privation or in broken homes were at risk. This reactionary backlash harkened back to the turn-of-the-century justice system, which was preoccupied with detecting pre-delinquency on the basis of social and cultural behaviour.

As Bradley (1994) points out, the resulting political debates about the Bulger murder called for more moral intervention, more classical punishment and an attack on liberal politics. But what is most clear is that the drama played out after the crime portrayed nihilistic criminal behaviour as being the result of a drift into immorality by the lower classes (with the attendant criminogens of pornography, alcohol and promiscuity), and liberal social policies were blamed.

By fictionalizing and exploiting the tragedy of the victim, the media, in concert with conservative politicians, were able to nurture a public panic that resulted in a call for more law and order and more intervention into the lives of marginalized families. Most noteworthy about this type of crime depiction is its ability to reconstruct and recontextualize the singular events of a case into a moralistic, societal framework in which moral breakdown, class privation and the devolution of family values are indicted. The oppressive potential of a highly classed society and the immorality of blaming and punishing the victim of economic forces is disregarded. The mechanism of this disregard is illustrated by the second strategy for producing crime accounts.

The Decontextualization of Crime

This second category of depictions illustrates how media reporting tends to remove crime from its socio-economic context and to recast it in moralistic and emotional frames of reference. The first example, from the *Montreal Gazette* (1989), is noteworthy for its blatant disregard for objectivity, its calculated attempt to create despair with the use of exaggeration and visually horrific images and, most importantly, its description of the events of a horrific youth crime in a businesslike manner.

The visual image from this *Montreal Gazette* article is obviously intended to represent youth in a particularly lethal context and provokes a visceral aversion to the young antagonist. The dark image is one of a competent young gunman, brandishing a weapon in a show of bravado. In addition, the first narrative we encounter is that of an incomprehensible act of youth violence.

> Four years ago Wednesday in a split-level home in the Toronto suburb of Scarborough, a 14-year-old boy armed with a .303-calibre rifle shot both his parents through the head as they slept.
>
> Then he shot his 7-year-old sister in the stomach as she watched morning cartoons on TV. The little girl bled to death in a chair in the living room, clutching her doll. (*Montreal Gazette* April 8, 1989:B1)

Several short paragraphs explain the crime in a detached police-style report, followed by unequivocal pronouncements that childhood crime is worse now than at any other time in Canadian history, a statement that is not only unsubstantiated but untrue (see Chapter 5).

> Children are committing more violent crimes than ever before in Canada and many believe that because of the Young Offenders Act, kids are getting away with murder—literally. (*Montreal Gazette* April 8, 1989:B1)

Any sense that there are other reasons for kids to commit crimes is left to the last few paragraphs of the rather lengthy article. The more even-handed discussions relating social inequality and lack of support services for marginalized kids is relegated to a truncated discussion at the end; the ideological potency of this article appears well before this.

This type of depiction removes the offense and the offender almost entirely from the socio-economic and legal context in which crimes occur. The producers of the message implicitly suggest that crime is a matter of inherent evil, that it is manifested in defiant, gun-wielding behaviour. By using alarmist un-truths—"the 12 to 17 year-old set is killing, raping, and assaulting more than ever before" (*Montreal Gazette,* April 8, 1989:B1)—the article creates, at the outset, a framework for reading the rest of the article.

The next article, Figure 3.1, although much shorter and more even-handed, also reads like a police report supplemented with speculations about crime and youth violence. In Chicago in September 1994 an eleven-year-old boy was murdered in a gangland-type slaying. The article in the news services (*Saskatoon Star Phoenix,* August 31, 1994:D12) concentrated on the child's affiliations with gang members, the types of crimes he had committed in his young career (including the gang-related murder of a fourteen-year-old girl) and the lamentations of community leaders who blamed the system for failing the child.

Figure 3.1. *Saskatoon Star Phoenix*, August 31, 1994:D12.

Murder suspect found in pool of blood

Chicago (AP)—His nickname was Yummy. In a short life filled with abuse, he was prosecuted at least eight times for robberies and other crimes before police suspected him of shooting one teenager dead and wounding two others.

Police started hunting for Robert Sandifur. They found him Thursday in a pool of blood beneath a railway overpass. He was 11.

His body—not yet five feet, not quite 70 pounds—lay about seven blocks from where police believe he opened fire Sunday at two different groups of boys, killing a 14-year-old girl, Shavon Dean, about 10 metres from her home.

Robert was suspected of having gang ties. Two gunshot wounds—one to the back of the head, one to the top—led police to suggest fellow gang members had killed him. Authorities had a suspect in the boy's slaying.

Solemn neighbors gathered around the pool of Robert's blood in the South Side neighborhood of neat yards and well-kept homes. Adults showed young children the wet blood as a warning.

"This is our problem," Valerie Jordan said. "The authorities and the system have failed. This is our child. The young lady that was killed, that was our baby."

In the last two years, Robert was prosecuted for robbery, car theft, arson and burglary. He was convicted twice and received probation, although one judge sentenced him to three weeks of detention for probation violations.

Robert was no stranger to the state's child welfare agency, either.

A 1986 investigation by the Department of Children and Family Services found scars on Robert's face, cordlike marks on his abdomen and leg, and cigarette burns on his buttocks.

Robert was taken from his mother and placed with his grandmother, who nicknamed him Yummy for his love of cookies. Complaints that she was not supervising the boy led to his placement in a juvenile facility in 1993, but he ran away.

In July, a judge returned Robert to his grandmother until the boy could be put in an out-of-state detention centre that permits children to be locked in or physically restrained, both of which are forbidden in Illinois.

Robert's grandmother, Janie Fields, became hysterical before she shut the door on reporters.

"I really can't say what I'm going through," she said. "but I know my baby's not here anymore and I can't say I love you Robert anymore."

Police Supt. Matt Rodriguez said the boy's death should send a message to other youths that "the promises of the gangs . . . are not promises of things that are good."

The article then changes abruptly to discuss a previous investigation by social services that revealed that the boy had been scarred by physical abuse and that social services had intervened. Subsequently, the article focuses on him being taken from his mother and placed in the care of his grandmother, who eventually relinquished custody to welfare agencies. The final words in the article, supplied by a local police superintendent, are a message to all youth that the promises of gangs often have fatal consequences.

The article evokes sympathy for the child offender/victim and laments the inability of the system to effectively care for him. But the article mostly concentrates on the family's pathology, the suggestion of broken homes headed by women and the implication that gangs are at the core of the criminal world. Although half-truths are present in the article, the major import occurs through omission. The article ignores the socio-economic context in which the child and his family dwell, the economic reality of social welfare agencies that are financially unable to carry out their mandates and the reality of industrialized societies that discard people to make a profit. What is missing in the journalistic analysis, besides the context of the crime, is the reality of this child as a survivor. It is remarkable in one sense that an eleven-year-old child could survive on the streets on his own. It is understandable that the only context for such survival is gang affiliations, when legitimate avenues of support fail. The struggle to survive is neither pathological nor indicative of a degenerating society; it is more likely a normal human response.

The most striking sentiment expressed here, and in fact in both articles, is that these deaths and the crimes that precipitated them, are indicative of a generation of children out of control. Both articles leave the reader with a sense of foreboding that nothing is to be done and that stricter crime-control measures, while not solutions, are the only possible reactions. The reader is left with reason for panic. Apparently nihilistic behaviour at such a young age is an affront to our collective desire to care for the young, for when the young are corrupted, the society must be morally self-destructive. The sense of pessimism inherent in such accounts is a powerful indication that nothing is working and that something corrective must be put into place. The insinuations are that the problems of youth are individual, family-based problems that need interven-tionist, punitive solutions rather than socio-economic support.

The Exception as the Rule: Truth and Expert Opinion

The third example, Figure 3.2, is from a 1994 issue of *Maclean's* magazine, the cover story of which is entitled "Kids Who Kill, Special Report" (Kaihla, DeMont and Wood 1994). The cover shows a young man holding a gun in a fashion that depicts his ability and familiarity with the weapon. Most striking about the picture, however, is the dress of the lethal youth, his jeans, t-shirt and inverted ball cap being icons of modern youth culture.

The article (Kaihla, DeMont and Wood 1994) discusses three Canadian

Figure 3.2. *Maclean's,* August 15, 1994, cover.

Kids Who Kill
Special Report: Why three young Canadians committed murder

Peter Bregg, Maclean's

cases in which young persons committed murder. The individual cases are presented in temporal and graphic detail and are accompanied by family photographs of the victims and their relatives, a grisly crime scene and one of the young offender in a prison garden. The articles concentrate on several dimensions of teenage criminality and imply that these levels of explanation are the most rational and fundamental and consequently offer the most hope for the control of deadly violence among youth.

The first suggestion is that youth crime is erratic and unpredictable and, by implication, is threatening to everyone. The article invokes expert medical testimony to attest to the psychotic inherent nature of these acts: youths like these—and the article stresses the ordinariness of their communities and activities—can be everywhere; psychopathic killers can be housed in the bodies of normal-appearing youth. The reader is left with the impression that a young killer (and youth criminals in general) could be the boy (and the article is extremely gendered) next door.

The second suggestion we see in the profiles of the three murders is part of its attempt to unpack and reconstruct the psychic lives of the young killers. The reports focus on outside influences such as exposure to pornography, the emulation of notorious movie criminals (the movie "Silence of the Lambs" is mentioned several times) and the dysfunction of family styles that included strict or lax discipline, absentee fathers, single motherhood and poverty. The ostensible markers of delinquency are introduced into the criminality equation as warning signs for pathological behaviour.

The preamble to the three case studies presents the "problem of youth crime" in language laden with sinister references to the unique predatory nature of the young killer. Further, the introduction offers a litany of inexplicable killings by children that have raised public pressure to reform the Young Offenders Act. The last paragraph in the article hypothesizes that what youth criminals have in common is a "stunning lack of empathy" for their victims. The article ends by calling on the work of an eminent psychiatrist to make sense of the youth crime wave; his conclusion is that more adolescents are now border-line personality types, "like the characters in the 'Silence of the Lambs'" (Kaihla, DeMont and Wood 1994:33), than in the past. Although the article attempts to be even-handed by explaining the position of those who argue for the lenient handling of young offenders, the overall journalistic slant is that the younger generation is nihilistic and state social-control mechanisms are not doing enough to curb the increasing youth violence in our society.

Overall, the article does present a compelling case for a continual attempt to understand and deal with youth killers. It would be impossible for anyone not to feel and share the extreme tragedy and loss felt by the victims and their relatives and communities. And, of course, there is a continuing need to protect people from harm. What the article transmits, however, is a sense of helpless-ness in the face of increasing homicides by youth that are characteristic of a degenerating youth culture. By invoking experts and their discourse, the article presents youth violence as unexceptional and commonplace and, by speculating on the origins of youth criminality, this type of discourse circulates moral indictments against family types, social classes and gendered environments. What we are left with, then, is a constructed world that is polarized into good and bad, where criminals are of a certain social caste, a world in which the answers to problems, once again, are to be found in law and order.

The Litany of Crime: Just the Facts

One of the ways that media portray the darkest side of youth crime is by drawing on a litany of official crimes in defense of the argument that "Teen violence is on the rise" (*Vancouver Sun,* September 19, 1992:A1). This extremely large headline is accompanied by a box entitled "A Year of Youth Mayhem," followed by a list of seven youth crimes presented in official police-report format. Quite clearly, the headline and list of crimes are intended to be the first things the reader sees. The same alarmist technique is used in the *Western Report* (1992:22). The headline reads "Youth Crime and Coddling," and it is accompanied by a picture of five youths walking in a mall in Edmonton. Under the picture is the subtitle "mall prowling." The inoffensive nature of a typical youth scene starkly contrasts with this offensive headline, which suggests that, when teens walk in a mall, they are prowling. This article is also accompanied by a large, boxed-off section entitled "Typical Teenage Terror," which is a chronological list of teen "crimes" that occurred in the Edmonton area. This litany of incidents is interesting in that rather severe crimes are interspersed with less severe acts of teenage deviance. The list gives the reader a sense of how reporters, while remaining within the boundaries of acceptable journalism, can create images that are both unethical and fear-mongering.

That these acts are criminal is not in question here. What is suspect, however, is the imputation that all of the acts are acts of terror and that all are typical teenage crimes. Official crime statistics show clearly that the majority of crimes teens are arrested and charged for are breaches of the YOA and defiance of the courts, minor acts of theft and vandalism, drug violations and minor assaults (cf. Chapter 5; Schissel 1995a; Winterdyk 1996). The litany of crimes is presented here as typical of a culture of terrorizing teenagers, and this message is reinforced by a picture of typical young males "prowling" in a mall, versus simply "hanging out somewhere." Interestingly, four of the ten crimes listed as "teenage terror" involve vehicle theft, debatable as a terrifying crime.

This terror over car theft points to an interesting phenomenon in the generalized panic over young offenders. The theft of adult property, especially a vehicle or the contents of a vehicle, creates public outrage as much or more than severe acts of violence. For example, the city of Regina has been embroiled in a battle with supposedly organized, young car thieves, dubbed the "Oldsmobile Gang." Although a pressing problem for police and civic officials, it is unlikely that this situation constitutes a crime wave of the proportion that we see in media presentations, especially given the fact that, since this ostensible "crime wave," further incidents have not occurred and the problem seems to have "resolved itself."

A final example, Figure 3.3, uses the same technique of bombarding the reader with a recital of crime but employs a somewhat different presentation to produce the same effect. The article, entitled a "A generation of outlaws: Wildly rising teen crime is blamed on a molly-coddle law" (*Alberta Report* 1991), begins with two depictions of teen crimes, one involving the robbery of a convenience store and one involving vandalism and automobile theft. What is most striking about the presentations is the inclusion of the victims' wishes and fears and testimonials by the police that the kids involved are completely out of control and unrepentant. The audience is essentially prepped for the forthcoming "facts."

A litany of crimes is presented after the sensationalized depictions have created an atmosphere of alarm and anger in the audience. In this instance, the list involves a series of official statistics for the province of Alberta that are contextualized in a discussion of increasing crime rates and numbers of chronic offenders. The focus of the "facts" are, once again, vehicle thefts, total crimes (without any explanation that most of these crimes are minor) and attendant commentary on the habitual nature of youth crime.

The technique of presenting a list of crimes and crime statistics is significant for several reasons. First, it forces the reader to view crimes that have taken place over a lengthy period in one visual frame, creating an illusion of a crime wave. Second, the list is compelling because it is not far removed from objective, empirical journalistic style—just the facts—except for some of the editorializing. Most importantly, though, this technique places crimes of various severity all under the same umbrella of terror. The end result is a snapshot of an historically disconnected "youth crime wave" compiled on the basis of official accounts.

Pictures and Headlines: What You See First Is What You Get

One of the most striking techniques the news media employ is the use of stark headlines and photo images to capture the attention of the reader and frame discussions in a predetermined ideological context. Television uses the technique of flash images and brief, out-of-context images to attract and capture the attention of the viewer (Postman 1994). The attraction of news on television is that it simplifies and condenses the news into something immediately understandable and yet immediately foreign and aversive. Television has been described as having a "primordial power" to profoundly shape public opinion. News on television is like a never-ending series of first impressions. And the impact of first impressions cannot be overstated for news reports like those exemplified by the articles that follow.

Figure 3.3. *Alberta Report*, February 24, 1992:18

A generation of outlaws
Wildly rising teen crime is blamed on a molly-coddle law

Grace and Kilung Ahn had already learned to distrust teenagers. Last September three 17-year-old thieves smashed their way into the couple's north-east Calgary confectionery, leaving with all the cigarettes they could carry. After two more late night break-ins in the following two months, the Ahns finally installed iron bars across the store's doors and windows. Still, Mrs. Ahn continued to look upon her home as a safe haven. But two weeks ago, robbers struck even there, scooping up $20,000 in cash the woman had diligently saved and stashed in a small plastic bag in her dresser.

The following day, police arrested two 17-year-olds for the crime, but not before the young men had gone on a 30-hour, $6,000 spree with the purloined loot. "They spent it on booze, fine hotel suites, ladies of the night, limos, clothes and drugs," says Calgary police staff sergeant Ron Oshanek. "They had a ball." They also had little fear of the possible penalties. One, in fact, was already on probation with the strict stipulation that he stay away from his accomplice. "The law has to change," says an angry Mrs. Ahn. "I wish they'd lock up teenagers. They take advantage of the easy laws."

That, no doubt, was also the feeling in Edmonton where teens engaged in a week-long crime spree. Two 14-year-old boys trashed a north-end Edmonton home, writing profanities on the walls and stealing everything of value. A 13-year-old boy who could barely see over the dashboard stole a car and rammed it into a snowbank. A 15-year-old snatched a vehicle from a junior high school parking lot, collided with a truck after ignoring a red light, and then was caught by four city fire fighters who gave chase when he fled the scene. Yet another 15-year-old crashed into a Co-op cab in a stolen car. And later that same night, two 14-year-old girls wound up in hospital, one in critical condition, after smashing a stolen pickup truck into two light poles following a police chase.

Yet it really wasn't that unusual a week, say police. Since the 1984 Young Offenders Act, teens have learned to love its "be easy on the kids" philosophy. That has led to a nation-wide surge in youth crime. The statistics are alarming:

• In 1991, Alberta vehicle thefts rose 42% over the previous year, reaching an all-time high of 7,023. Edmonton police constable Pete Draganiuk says auto theft today is what shoplifting was to students a generation ago. Almost 80% of car thieves are under 18, and part of the game involves fleeing from the police.

• In Calgary each year 6,000 teens, almost 10% of all city kids aged 12 to 17, become involved in the juvenile justice system. Charges against young offenders for violent crimes, such as assaults, sexual offenses and murders, almost doubled from 486 in 1988 to 871 in 1990.

• One quarter of all juvenile charges in Calgary are laid against a group of only 125 chronic habitual offenders, says the city's police superintendent Gerry Baxter. Most are 16 and 17 years old, and would have been treated as adults under the law before passage of the Young Offenders Act. "These habitual offenders have attained a wealth of experience in the world of crime," he says, adding that they have no fear of the system.

The first example is probably the most stark. The article was the cover story for the July 31 edition of *Alberta Report*. I have included the magazine cover (Figure 3.4), the cover story description in the table of contents (Figure 3.5) and the first page of the article (Figure 3.6) to provide the reader with a sense of the graphic and exploitative design of the article.

The image on the cover is blatant and unapologetic. It is one of a criminal-looking girl, adorned with several earrings, brandishing a weapon with an obvious inclination to shoot. And the first sentiment we see is that feminism and the liberation of women are directly responsible for a boom in violent youth crime led by girls. On the contents page, we see a brief abstract of the cover story, retitled "Killer girls." It is here where journalistic licence becomes supplanted by abject bias and distortion.

The brief description asserts that the "latest crop" of teenage girls (thus, all teenage girls by implication) can be as "malicious" and "evil" as the boys (again, all boys by implication). Further, the synopsis declares an explosion in youth crime—against the abundance of evidence to the contrary. And, finally, feminism and the struggle for gender equality is indicted as criminogenic.

The first page of the cover story shows the same gun-wielding girl with a headline that reads "You've come a long way, baby: prodded by feminism, today's teenaged girls embrace antisocial male behaviour." The messages are clear and repetitive. As readers search for the article on page 24, they are besieged with a series of deliberate images and messages that frame the discussion in a framework of loathing that borders on hate literature.

The next example is much more subtle in its presentation, but it also uses visual emphasis to highlight and frame the vitriolic argument of the article. The May 1993 edition of *Chatelaine* produced an article on youth crime and justice that was based on the premise that youth are an identifiable subculture that is evolving into a counterculture in defiance of adult society. The first page of the article is framed with a glaring sentiment that occupies one-third of the page. The statement reads:

> Violent-crime charges against kids have more than doubled in five years. Does this mean we are raising a generation of weapon-bearing head-smashing monsters? An encounter with one young felon leads Patricia Pearson to explore the dark side of teen culture.(*Chatelaine* 1993:74)

Figure 3.4: *Alberta Report,* July 1995, cover.

Figure 3.5. *Alberta Report,* July 31, 1995:1.

Killer girls

Girls, it used to be said, were made of sugar and spice. Not anymore. The latest crop of teenage girls can be as violent, malicious and downright evil as the boys. In fact, they're leading the explosion in youth crime. It's an unexpected byproduct of the feminist push for equality.

Figure 3.6. *Alberta Report,* **July 31, 1995:24.**

You've come a long way, baby
Prodded by feminism, today's teenaged girls embrace antisocial male behavior

Courtney Love, rock's fastest rising star and acclaimed "den mother" to millions of adoring teenage fans, is also an unrivalled tough slut. The "Great White Widow" of the late rock icon, drug addict and celebrated suicide, Kurt Cobain is raunchy enough to make faded pop "bad girl" Madonna Ciccone mossy with envy. "You're *guuuuut—le—ess!"* Ms. Love retches repeatedly above the screaming guitars of her band, known as Hole. The band's platinum CD *Live Through This* was crowned 1994's best album by *Rolling Stone* magazine. "You can try to suck me dry, but there's nothing left to suck," the tortured grunge queen with the testosterone fixation moans on her "Gutless" ballad. "Just you try to hold me down. Come on try to shut me up."

If mothers have always observed the unfamiliar pursuits of their adolescent daughters with mingled suspicion and anxiety, they have good reason to feel nauseated today. Impelled by contemporary culture, their daughters are becoming not just difficult, but often violent and ruthless monsters. That was dramatically highlighted earlier this month, when three Calgary girls were charged in the brutal stabbing death of a Calgary man.

Modern women may have no one to blame but themselves, however. Girls, after all, are only following their foremothers' lead in seizing the torch of the 1970s' feminist cults of androgyny and victimhood and torquing it up to new extremes. And as they abandon traditional feminine domains for once-masculine arenas like commerce and politics, they are increasingly emulating less savoury male models—such as murderers and maimers.

The statement is obviously intended to precipitate interest in the rest of the article. On the next page we see another statement set off in large letters in the middle of the text that reads: "Teenagers like intimidating people. They like the power, it makes them feel good" (*Chatelaine* 1993:75). For the viewer who casually thumbs through the magazine, these statements are impossible to miss and, although the text may be more even-handed in its understanding of the problem of youth crime, the implications of the visual stimuli are clear and pointed. By presenting a rhetorical question in graphic and value-laden language—"weapon-bearing, head-smashing monsters"—the reader is left with the impression that the possibility exists that the entire *generation* is headed in a terrifying direction. The article suggests that violent crime charges have more than doubled in five years without commenting on what changes in the practice of justice and policing may have prompted such increases. These decontextualized statements appear as truths. Thorough reading of the whole article, however, shows that these sentiments must be qualified and contextualized.

The second statement—"teenagers like intimidating people"—reads like an axiomatic truth. As we read in the article, this statement was made by one police officer in Ottawa as he speculates on why teenagers engage in violence. Obviously, a subjective comment, its out-of-context use in large, bold print creates an ideological framework for reading the article—if the article will be read. If not, the cursory reader will be exposed to only this "visceral truth." And that "truth" is that teenagers are intimidating and power hungry—overall, an alarmist statement about the human condition.

Like television images on the evening news, the two stark verbal images on the first two pages of the article are intended for quick consumption. Like television, as well, the statements are unambiguous in their indictment of youth and presents a clear, bifurcated and ultimately consumable sentiment.

A last example of the use of television-like images appeared in the *Maclean's* August 15, 1994 issue (Kaihla, DeMont and Wood 1994). The cover story was entitled "Kids Who Kill," which was emboldened in unusually large letters on a picture of a young man wearing a ball cap backwards and holding a handgun in a ready position (see Figure 3.2). I discussed this article previously in this chapter but turn to it again to discuss the visual techniques that article employs. The article is based on the circumstances surrounding three particularly inexplicable and horrible murders by youths. Notwithstanding the rare and selected nature of the portrayals, the article is noteworthy in its use of photographic images and large lettering to present a viewpoint consistent with the horrific cases. The cover portrays the potential young killer in typical youth dress. Without the gun, the portrait is of any young man and the point is reinforced in the article that a young killer or assailant could easily be the "boy next door." This photo is reproduced on the opening two pages of the article, covering more than 50 percent of the space. And "Kids Who Kill" is emblazoned again, in even larger letters, over the picture.

The visuals lead into the stories of the three murders and include a picture of a child victim, members of victims' families and the police inspecting a blood-soaked crime scene. Each story is accompanied by a large, red headline that reinforces the sentiment that these killers are like "the boy across the road" and their crimes are a "family affair." Overall, the photographs and headlines occupy 30–50 percent of each page. It is amazing how similar these pictures and headlines are to the visual flashes on television news programs. This is as much a photo-essay as a news article.

Evil Incarnate: The Nature of Kids

One of the most blatant techniques the media use to build an image of offensive youths is that of declarations, often endorsed by professional experts, that children are inherently evil and that youth misconduct is the result of uncontrolled natural impulses. The ideological message is that these inherently vile beings need strict family discipline or, failing that, require strict institutional intervention. Most depictions of horrific crimes are framed in this type of nature versus nurture discourse, in which nature seems to win out.

The first example of this appeared in the previously mentioned *Chatelaine* (1993:74, 75) article. In addition to the condemnatory headlines addressing the "Dark Side of Teen Culture," the article offers that teenagers, as a generic group, "like intimidating people." The article, somewhat less blatant in its attack on the nature of youth than the headline, discusses some of the reasons why youth engage in antisocial behaviour but constantly returns to an "outlaw" teen culture that is collectively defiant of the "accepted rituals of the society." Finally the article declares that, because of society's inability to isolate the primary cause of teenage misconduct, "isolating each cause is no better than describing individual parts of an elephant—you don't account for the nature of the beast." "Nature" and "beast" references leave little doubt in the reader's mind that biology produces the evil animal, and this didactic position is visually reinforced with large, alarmist headlines.

A second example of inflammatory attacks on youth uses a cover page with the picture of a child from the neck down in handcuffs. The cover story, entitled "Junior gone wild: An aging do-your-own-thing generation lashes out at its savage offspring" (*Alberta Report*, May 9, 1994), is followed by the lead article entitled "Locking up the wild generation" (again in large, dark type). The article is typical in its presentation of a litany of alarming violent crimes perpetrated by youth and its professed frustration with being unable to explain such behaviour. Like most doctrinal attacks on youth, the visual/verbal referents are to a generic youth culture that is savage by nature.

A third article tries to understand what it is about youth that predisposes them to antisocial behaviour; the answer, expressed in large headlines and in testimonials embedded in the text is "boredom." The article, entitled "Teen Violence: Murder, Mayhem have their Roots in Boredom" (*Calgary Herald*, April 18, 1995:A5), presumes at the outset that "boredom is very frustrating for all of us, particularly for the young" and psychologizes that boredom inspires thrill-seeking behaviour that results in violence. The article then lists a series of senseless violent acts and culminates in a discussion that says serial killers were once bored teenagers. What the story conveys, initially with its stark headline and finally with its connection between boredom and serial murder, is that teenagers "will create provocative circumstances to gain their kicks and rid themselves of the burden of boredom," and that boredom is potentially lethal, but only to adolescents.

Interestingly, references to boredom and teenage pathology most often occur with reference to ordinary, middle-class teenagers as potential murderers, as the following two examples illustrate. In an article entitled "Kids next door could be violent" (*Calgary Herald*, May 11, 1992:A1, A2), an expert describes the ordinary nature of youth violence: "psychiatrist Parsons fears, it will breed more bored, contemptuous kids who need to be shaken back into reality . . . we are seeing average kids who have no respect for themselves or for society." In a similar article entitled "I Am Gavin: How a bright kid with excellent self-esteem slaughtered his whole family" (*Alberta Report*, December 6, 1993:18), the author laments that "human beings are by nature selfish creatures."

Testimonials to the naturalness of youth violence are found most often in articles about teenage murderers. Even without directly talking about an innate violent nature for teenagers, such articles promote the suggestion that murder may be an ordinary activity for kids that can result from such normally innocuous psychological states as selfishness, high or low self-esteem and the need for thrills. In the *Maclean's* article entitled "Kids Who Kill" (Kaihla, DeMont and Wood 1994), the three cases described in detail are typically about "The boy across the road," "A young killer who looked like a choirboy and who had not obvious problems at home" and a "handsome, rather lanky youth" that an adult trusted so completely that "later that night he left the teen to babysit his own two young sons." The three descriptions suggest that youth murder occurs in ordinary socio-economic contexts. The same type of writing occurs in an article in the *Alberta Report* (December 6, 1993:20). This article, entitled "Crimes Beyond Reason," lists five cases of teenagers who killed family members and begins the discussions by suggesting that "ever since Cain slew Abel, humanity has harboured men, women, and children who can, without real reason or remorse, strike down those they love the most." The descriptions are once again rife with references to kids acting violently while engaged in little more than petty theft or in reaction to parental discipline, all the while communicating the feeling that ordinary kids will kill for trivial reasons.

This final list of media references provides further evidence that we fear the inborn wickedness of children:

> We live in a society where very dangerous weapons are available. Most kids are subject to impulse, and that often results in something deadly." (*Montreal Gazette*, July 18, 1993:C1)

> You have someone entering puberty in a high state of arousal, confusion, with the hormones percolating. They are very, very susceptible especially if they're from an unstable background. (*Calgary Herald*, August 9, 1990:C3).

> [P]sychologist William Coulson . . . [t]o his way of thinking, [believes

that] low self-esteem is not the root cause of youth crime. Indeed, part of the problem may be too much self-esteem. Adolescents need to be told what is right and wrong, because they are not rationally capable of deciding for themselves. Children should not trust their impulses. (*Alberta Report*, May 9, 1994:37)

Teenagers feel carefree and indestructible. They live in the present. (*Globe and Mail*, November 19, 1992:A8).

Conclusion

The examples analyzed above illustrate the different ways that public discourse has been framed in newspapers and magazines. What is most important in analyzing moral panics is how these accounts of criminal behaviour use individual examples as the norm, and how the criminal behaviour is decontextualized from the structured nature of society. When crimes are framed in the context of morality, poor parenting and "poor people," the problem is reduced to the level of individual pathology and its moral connections to privation; the legitimacy of "normal," affluent lifestyles is reinforced, as is the legitimacy of the social order. In fact, the moral panic draws on existing public perceptions about crime and criminality and reinforces these beliefs by foment-ing fear about the unpredictable and increasingly dangerous nature of youth activity.

In essence, the real connection between poverty and youth crime is not individual pathology but the fact that the marginalized are more vulnerable to commit certain stereotypical crimes (street crime, primarily) and more vulner-able to the scrutiny and control of the criminal justice system. We, as a society, need to ensure that resources for marginalized kids are available because, as Monture-Angus (1996) argues, there is a distinction between disadvantaged and dispossessed. The problems of dispossessed or marginalized kids, like those described in this book, are economic and not moral. In a similar vein, Monture-Angus argues, for example, that people in Aboriginal communities tend to be relatively poor and unemployed and yet they maintain a strong sense of community. I would argue, on the basis of my research, that the same can be said for dispossessed youth in general. In fact, as discussed in Chapter 7, youths tend to be loyal and generous, and have a strong sense of solidarity with one another. Their lived reality is, however, that they are caught more often than kids who are more affluent and mainstream.

In terms of the effects of media images of marginalized youth, although there is an argument that people do not passively accept what they see and read carte blanche, they may, in fact, use accounts and representations in their own ways. On the contrary, though, what this book shows, I believe, is that the groups who dominate the media—white, male, professional, capitalist classes—hold hateful, stereotypical views of youth misconduct. Further, when they present these views, they obliterate other, more favourable images of youth. At the same time, they make it appear that there is no alternative to youth crime other than "tough" law and order. Those who dominate, in effect, circumscribe the public debate about youth and the troubles they face.

Chapter 4

The Socio-Fiction of Young Folk Devils

When the media write about youth crime and misconduct, they generally attack those who are disempowered and marginalized or write in the context of the lives of such people. In so doing, they help create and foster a collective enmity towards young who are already socially and economically disabled. The disadvantage that racial minorities, women and the poor suffer at the hand of socio-economic and socio-legal systems is indeed exacerbated by media accounts of crime. William Ryan, in his landmark study entitled *Blaming the Victim,* states that "difference is in itself hampering and maladaptive. The Different Ones are seen as less competent, less skilled, less knowing—in short less human" (1976:10).

Ryan's (1976) work constantly reminds us that the already victimized are the most likely to be isolated for negative labelling. Groups that are most vulnerable are those who are the least likely to be able to resist public enmity because they are easily distinguishable from the dominant socio-economic strata. When we look at typical depictions of youth criminals in the media, it becomes readily apparent that the categories for condemnation are consistent: poor families (living in poor communities), racially-based gangs and groups (made up of recent immigrants or Aboriginal Canadians), and both single mothers and mothers who work outside the home. The categories of class, race and gender often arise in sociological analyses as the categories upon which discrimination and maltreatment are thrust, and the discursive creation of youth folk devils is no exception. In accounts of youth deviance, however, race and class often become the identifiers and code words for gang criminality, and class and gender for criminogenic families.

Many of the depictions I analyze in this book border on hate literature. As an analytical device, I would ask you to substitute mainstream and powerful racial, socio-economic and gender categories for those already present. This technique should illustrate to you that hateful statements are only tolerated when directed at outgroups.

Vile Womanhood: Sugar and Spice and Everything Evil

Some of the most overt and most subtle forms of hatred are directed at women and motherhood. Most of the depictions, however, are couched in circumspect language that often laments the states of privation in which many people live. When one looks deeper, the subtle images and messages nevertheless imply that, while poverty may not be a matter of choice, single mothers are responsible for their socio-economic and marital conditions and that ultimately they are the most likely to produce criminal children through their own negligence. Rarely does the account mention the responsibility of the father, the society in which women's work is devalued and underpaid, or the underfunded system of social justice that herds kids in and out in an attempt to cope with diminishing resources. The offenders and victims are quite distinct, and mothers who live below the poverty line are clearly constructed as inadvertent or deliberate offenders.

The first category of depictions is based on surprisingly even-handed descriptions of life for young offenders. These presentations focus on trying to understand the social and personal origins of youth crime, and in this regard seem to be quite progressive in their approaches. The hidden messages, however, come to light as the articles venture further into the realm of personal responsibility for crime. I have used the following article in Chapter 3 but present an excerpt of it here to illustrate how an article can attempt to present a factual accounting for crime but ultimately place the blame for criminal behaviour on the most vulnerable people in society. Further, the article omits any discussion of the structural origins of problem kids by focusing on abuse within the home without discussing why abuse occurs and why dysfunctional families exist below the poverty line.

> Any child can kill, but there is a disturbing trend among those who do. They are often abused, neglected or unwanted. Their homes are run more like hotels with parents not bothering if they check in or out. They wander the streets and wind up stealing car stereos or burglarizing homes—often because there's nothing better to do. They don't express their feelings, they grow up seeing people as objects and they can't differentiate right and wrong. And then they kill. (*Calgary Herald*, August 9, 1990:C3)

This article presents an alarmingly stereotypic view of youth crime. The chronological listing of the steps in the development of criminal behaviour reads like a psychiatrist's report, preceded by the alarmist and absurd statement that any child can kill. One thing necessarily leads to another, which leads to another patterned response, which leads to an emotional flatness that leads to murder. In this development of the killer's personality, the blameworthy are without question the families who don't want their children, don't care where they are and abuse them. These stereotypes are plentiful in news reports and, as I will show, they are often wrong.

The article then presents a short list of murders by youth and culminates with a statement by unspecified "experts":

> Criminologists and psychologists agree that raising a child who kills can happen to families from all walks of life, but families that are barely surviving—the welfare mom in East Vancouver, the newly arriving immigrant to Surrey—are more likely to see it in their homes. (*Calgary Herald,* August 9, 1990:C3)

Here is where the article draws on public fears and stereotypes to make its point. The criminogenic families are single mothers and immigrants. The not-so-subtle implication is that these families produce killers, for that is what the article is about. Bold statements such as this are not only untrue and unsupported, they are sexist and racist in their indictment of women and immigrants. The article finishes with a powerful statement by an unidentified criminologist who implies that all teenagers are potentially criminal: "You have someone in a high state of arousal, confusion, with the hormones percolating. They are very, very susceptible especially if they're from an unstable background" (*Calgary Herald,* August 9, 1990:C3). The article has come full circle from an opening statement about the human condition that any child can kill, to a similar biodeterminist avowal that puberty and hormonal changes create lethal kids, especially among kids who live in poverty.

The James Bulger case in England is one I have also used in a previous chapter, and I refer to it again because it illustrates how media accounts attempt to be fair-minded by presenting an abundance of possible reasons for why horrific crimes occur. But, like most articles on young offenders, the discussion focuses on mothers and families as the root of youth evil. This is typical in the predictable media construction of a case of pure evil and its attendant social implications.

As Bradley (1994:10) argues, "The Bulger murder was not a symbol of nineties Britain; but the media reaction to it was." In typical sensationalist fashion, London newspapers went on a rampage of speculation as to the connections between this horrific youth crime and underclass, female-headed families. The stories concentrated on a mother with seven children who smoked, dyed her hair, drank and had boyfriends.

One of the children was described as "the classic product of a broken home' (*Daily Mail,* November 25, 1993). The implication in the London papers was that children left to single mothers (or families with absentee fathers) are potential killers. The most harmful sentiment to arise from these anti-mother accounts of youth crime is that society needs to be vigilant in watching for signs of criminality. And the British papers provided the markers of family criminality, including single-motherhood, divorce or separation, poverty and parents who indulge in vices. In fact, the two boys who killed Bulger were not at all typical of children of separated or divorced parents.

Much of the indictment of mothers and women in crime accounts is based on our belief in our ability to detect pre-criminality, or *pre-delinquency,* a term that was coined in the early decades of twentieth-century Canada to refer to children who were at risk of breaking the law on the bases of their social and economic characteristics (Schissel 1993:9). Importantly, the search for pre-delinquency goes on. David Farrington, a British criminologist, was quoted as saying that "children likely to become juvenile delinquents or adult criminals can often be identified as early as eight or nine" (*Vancouver Sun,* February 26, 1987:9). Like the rhetoric of times past, Farrington argues that:

> those who turned into criminals were more likely to come from deprived, low-income families in slum housing. Those who turned later to a life of crime also tended to have low intelligence and do poorly in school, had parents with poor child-rearing skills who used harsh or erratic discipline. (*Vancouver Sun,* February 26, 1987:9)

The next example illustrates how criminality is linked to poor parenting, which is linked to poverty and single-motherhood, which is ultimately linked to immorality. The article from *Western Report* (August 31, 1992:25) is entitled "The age outside the law: Three young boys turn a town upside down and nobody can touch them." The story is about a nine-year-old and two eight-year-olds who confessed to starting a fire under a trailer that resulted in its loss. The article goes on to discuss how kids under twelve are "completely" immune from the law and social services. And, like many articles on youth crime, the Young Offenders Act is at the centre of the controversy for being too lenient on child offenders. Most importantly, and most distressingly, the article suggests time and again that the spate of crimes in this particular community is, although unsubstantiated, the product of kids out of control. And the pictures accompanying the article are obvious in their focus on the pre-criminals as being Native and the victims as being non-Native.

The caption under one photo uses the term "pre-criminals," and the article speculates on the social background of the typical pre-criminal. And once again we see blatant references to family breakdown: "This town has one of the highest rates of divorce and busted-up families in all of Alberta . . . young children, many of single-parent families, pack the 7-11 store on the main drag long after midnight" (*Western Report* 1992:25). The alarm generated by this article comes on two fronts. First, the startling implication is that because these children are "outside the law," they and their families can victimize at will and be protected by the law. Second, the children are very young, are products of broken homes headed by mothers and had no sense of right or wrong—they were "oblivious to the damage done"—although they maintained that the fire was accidental and they cried when they confessed to the police.

Another example, a headline in the *Vancouver Sun* (April 16, 1993:A4) produces a similar sentiment, although the ensuing article is unusually unbiased and fair in its presentation. The headline reads "Defiance of the Law Brings Claim Young Offenders Act Too Limited: It's Outrageous Behaviour by Outrageous Children Probably Raised by Outrageous Parents." Before the reader gets to the substance of the argument within the text, the article is framed in a context of outrageous children and outrageous parents. As most studies illustrate, most youth misconduct is neither outrageous nor unusual, nor the result of outrageous parents, especially single parents, unless, of course, we consider privation and marginalization as outrageous.

I wish now to return to the cover story in *Alberta Report* (July 31, 1995) discussed previously to recall the visual depiction of a young girl brandishing a gun beside a title that reads "Killer girls." The visual nature of the account aside, the article is significant in its flagrant indictment of women's struggle for gender equality, which is declared to be at the core of criminality, and how this blatantly prejudicial narrative is given credibility by invoking the statements of those who should be most upset by the absurdities therein.

> If mothers have always observed the unfamiliar pursuits of their adolescent daughters with mingled suspicion and anxiety, they have good reason to feel nauseated today. Impelled by contemporary culture, their daughters are becoming not just difficult, but often violent and ruthless monsters. That was dramatically highlighted earlier this month, when three Calgary girls were charged in the brutal stabbing death of a Calgary man. . . . Modern women may have no one to blame but themselves, however. Girls, after all, are only following their foremothers' lead in seizing the torch of the 1970's feminist cults of androgyny and victimhood and torquing it up to new extremes. And as they abandon traditional feminine domains for once-masculine arenas like commerce and politics, they are increasingly emulating less savory male models—such as murderers and maimers. As American feminist novelist Katherine Dunn unapologetically puts it: "Being equal means being equally bad and equally good." (*Alberta Report, July 31,* 1995:24)

This article is especially noteworthy for its attempts to link criminality with the "dark side" of femaleness, the unnatural desire to be like men. The article is framed around a "cult of female violence" whose spokeswomen are Courtney Love and Roseanne Barr. By posing two show-business people as icons of the modern violent woman, the article indicts images of women who are in control and who defy traditional female roles, even though in the case of Love and Barr the defiance is most certainly done for entertainment value. The accompanying pictures show grunge rock singer Love in a seductive, defiant pose with the caption "Tormented Trollop Love: Driven by Testosterone" (*Alberta Report,*

July 31, 1995:27). In the case of TV sitcom star Barr, the camera has captured her in a particularly evil-looking pose with a caption that reads "Roseanne: Just Call Me a Killer Bitch" (*Alberta Report,* July 31, 1995:27). Although the article seems unable or unwilling to admit that these are contrived media images that bare little resemblance to real-life, it is callous in its barrage of statements regarding the male-like nature of bad girls. Love is "the tortured grunge queen with the testosterone fixation," and Barr says "I think women should be more violent, kill more of their husbands"(*Alberta Report,* July 31, 1995:27). The imputation is that Love and Barr are feminists who condone violence. More important than these almost silly references to media personages, whose motivation is popularity, are the hateful references in this article to Love as an "unrivalled tough slut," to her singing as "retching" and to her as a trollop; these are indications of the lengths to which magazines and newspapers will go to seduce readers. Furthermore, the inflammatory language in the article is typical in that it is intended to raise aversive passions in the reader, to engender an unquestioning belief that we are on a march to self-destruction and that violent teens are the torch bearers.

Finally the article reinforces its arguments through varied and bizarre testimonials that, for the reader, all but prove that what is being said is incontrovertible. Authors, identified as feminist commentators, are quoted, quite out of context, at various places throughout the article, lamenting that traditional femaleness is dying:

> [T]oday's teenagers are rejecting their female nature altogether. They have turned against the idea of what it is to be a woman; women are not sequestered in their kitchens as they used to be. As a result our crimes are no longer limited to poisoning our husbands and abusing our children. We can hitchhike across the country killing people. We can drive off on an armed robbery spree. (*Alberta Report,* July 31, 1995:24)

The president of the Canadian Police Association is quoted as saying that although females in general have achieved equality, the downside of that is that they are much more active in crime. Both statements are unsubstantiated and inaccurate claims. The article explains that such an outcome was not an entirely unexpected consequence of female emancipation, and in a rather outlandish addition to the litany of professional testimonials, the article quotes Queen Victoria:

> "Woman would be the most hateful, heartless and disgusting of human beings were she allowed to unsex herself," the British monarch wrote in an 1870 letter. Her prediction has been borne out, Mr. Racho acknowledges ruefully: "It is sad to note how each advance seems to

make women more unsatisfied, more spiteful, and more vulgar."(*Alberta Report,* July 31, 1995:25)

With this preamble the article goes on to explain that "[i]ndeed some of the crimes by modern girls seem every bit as vulgar as any perpetrated by men" (*Alberta Report,* July 31, 1995:25). And using the technique of providing a list of cases that proves the point, the article describes a series of schoolyard incidents involving violence and the voices of young male counterparts affirming that "females can outdo the most savage male" (*Alberta Report,* July 31, 1995:25).

Articles such as this make a connection between the struggle for gender equality and youth crime and, thereby, indict strong women as a social evil. The implications are clear and rather common: that women who choose to go outside of the home are a social risk, that mothers are mostly responsible for child rearing and are to blame when children go wrong, that there is an unpredictable natural female essence, that traditional femininity is lost when calculating women decide to shrug off their natural familial duties and that, if we wish to detect pre-delinquency, we had better study the home and especially the quality and degree of maternal care.

A final example illustrates how media accounts foster ideas of traditional parenthood and indict mothers, especially mothers without husbands, and feminist qualities as potentially harmful to kids. I have chosen to include this paragraph in its entirety because of its twisted logic, because the article is completely oblivious to the connections between dominating fathers and family violence and because of the use of a named but unidentified generic professor. The absurdity of the article and the subtle disdain for mothers and mothering is self-evident:

> The presence of a father in the home is especially important, Professor Coulson says, because "children need someone in residence whom they fear. Yes, fathers must be caring and loving and friendly, but we shouldn't forget their power to invoke fear in their children." By allowing their role to become feminized, he argues, fathers have lost some of this power. The result is "children with mushy identities," according to Professor Coulson. These types of kids "are available to become anything their peers want them to be," and have trouble resisting the temptation to be dishonest or criminal. (*Alberta Report,* May 2, 1994:39)

If violence begets violence, then families like those described above will surely produce it.

Youth Gangs: Race and Running with the Pack

The "Killer girls" example I used in the preceding section is spotted throughout with references to gangs. And, like most media articles, the word "gang" is never defined but is used loosely to refer to kids who "hang around" in twos or threes and have an identifiable ethnicity or class. In fact, this article relates an incident in which a girl in Edmonton was "surrounded by 10 native girls who pushed her to the ground, kicked her and punched her in the face and stole her leather bomber jacket"(*Alberta Report*, July 31, 1995:25).

The panic over gangs that is typified by this article has been well-documented, especially in British research. Cohen's (1980) landmark work alerted us to the prospect that public actors such as politicians, business people and the media have the potential to define, identify and scapegoat relatively vulnerable, highly identifiable people. For my purposes, there are two important issues in media discourse surrounding gangs: (1) the potential terror that resides in kids "hanging around in groups," a phenomenon that is, ironically, very typical of adult society; and (2) the imputed relationships between gangs, specifically gang violence, and racialized or immigrant groups.

A typical example of how the press, in compliance with the police and courts, overreacts to and exaggerates teenage gang activity and imputes such activity to visible minorities occurred in Saskatoon in October 1995. The city police issued a press release suggesting that criminal gangs were becoming a problem in the city and that these gangs were racially-based and composed of relatively young people. The initial press release estimated that twelve gangs existed in the city and were engaged in drug use and the sex trade; the alarm was sounded that the police did not have the staff or the skills to deal with the situation. After police and civic officials were visited by a youth-gang specialist from Winnipeg, the *Saskatoon Star Phoenix* carried an article that discussed police estimates that at least twelve organized youth gangs could be identified in Saskatoon and that their activities were restricted to the downtown core. The article, entitled "Street Gangs Reality in City" (*Saskatoon Star Phoenix*, November 4, 1995:A1, A2), argued that much of the evidence for the gang presence includes graffiti advertising "gang-related" sentiments and an increase in sports-jackets thefts. Much of the article expressed uncertainty surrounding gang activity and speculated on the danger of gangs reaching maturity in the city. The article caused a good deal of public furor and prompted civic and police officials to form a police task force to pre-empt gang violence.

The report illustrates how journalists use speculation and half-truths to create an atmosphere of alarm, while inserting a series of disclaimers that indicate the information may not be true. Consider the chronology of presentations in this article and how they create an aura of fact from uncertain information. The article begins:

Indian Posse. White Supremacists. Cowboys. Indie Boys. West Side

Divas. Luckys. Flips. These are street-gang names, and they're not from Los Angeles or New York. Nor are they from Vancouver or Toronto. And they're not from Calgary or Winnipeg either. They're from Saskatoon." (*Saskatoon Star Phoenix,* November 4, 1995)

The writer suggests that at least seven organized gangs exist in Saskatoon. Later on in the article the detractions begin:

> The full extent of street-gang activity in the city is an open question. . . . All that remains of gangs in the downtown corridor now is the distinctive graffiti sprayed on brick walls and written on doorways. . . . The police will not publicly confirm the names of the gangs for fear of legitimizing something that may not exist. . . . There are wildly divergent estimates of how many gang members are on the streets in Saskatoon. They range from in the low 20s to as many as 300. (*Saskatoon Star Phoenix,* November 4, 1995)

Quite unapologetically, this article, in both the title and the opening statements, presents a social problem as established fact and then later distances itself from the assertion. A few weeks later, after the panic had subsided, the *Saskatoon Star Phoenix* (December 2, 1995:A8) printed an article based on new evidence from the police force that there were at most only two gangs in Saskatoon, they were loosely organized, they likely didn't have ties to organized crime and they did not pose a significant policing problem. An unsubstantiated alarm over youth crime had raised the public's fear, had for a short time created a reality that preoccupied local citizens, had condemned local inner city youth but was ultimately found to be spurious. This example illustrates how a public alarm over youth crime can arise quickly, that the press is significant in fostering such panics and that people tend to dismiss the lies and exaggerations as harmless mistakes.

Several other things were noteworthy in this series of events. First, the police were fulfilling their mandate to be prepared against threats to public safety. In their enthusiasm to do the right thing, they sounded an alarm that reverberated throughout the community and, in their desire to adequately warn the public, they flagrantly exaggerated the extent of gang violence. Second, by focusing on the downtown area, the police, as is often the case with the youth justice system, turned the problem of gang violence into one of geography, race and class. Like all typical, relatively affluent Canadian cities, Saskatoon's youth violence, gang membership and vandalism and graffiti are not restricted to inner city areas. In fact, the affluent areas of such cities also report rather high levels of defiant and deviant behaviours among youth. Like all moral panics, however, the targets of the community's collective hostility were marginalized, inner city, ethnically identifiable youth. Ultimately, "gang" becomes a racist code word in the media to refer to Aboriginal and immigrant kids. Third, the press was more than willing to partake of the debate, illustrating an essential quality of a thriving moral panic, i.e., cooperation between the media and agencies of social control. Lastly, it is significant that the claims regarding youth crime and gang membership gained credibility after the debate was endorsed by the presence of experts. Whether or not experts know or understand the singular circumstance, their opinions on a wider range of topics suggest that the concern must be legitimate. The expert on gangs in this case addressed issues of organized crime, the exploitation of children and the culture of gangs, all topics that have currency and relevancy in Canadian society. That these issues are important and deserving of public attention is not in dispute. The expert opinion in question, however, by being presented in an atmosphere of general paranoia about young offenders, shifted the focus from adult crime and issues of child welfare to young gang members. Once again, it is conceivable that the best intentions of public officials and social control agents resulted in a constructed malevolence for young people.

Headlines from newspapers in other civic jurisdictions illustrate similar tendencies to overstate the youth gang menace. The headlines are pointed: "Teen Gangs Attractive to Students" (*Winnipeg Free Press,* April 14, 1993:B2, B8); "Youth Gang Violence on Rise: Toronto Schools, Police Urge Community to Act" (*Globe and Mail,* May 23, 1990:A1, A2); "Street Gangs a Reality in City" (*Saskatoon Star Phoenix,* November 4, 1995:A1). One of the obvious journalistic techniques—or incompetencies—employed in articles exemplified by the above is the generic use of the word "gang" to refer to any situation that involves more than one young person. Some of the articles discuss organized gangs with racialized or gendered names such as "Indian Posse. White Supremacists. . . . Indie Boys" (*Saskatoon Star Phoenix,* November 3, 1995:A1) the "Nasty Girls, the Nigger Posse" (*Maclean's,* May 18, 1992:35).

Furthermore, reports include sweeping, unsubstantiated but condemnatory statements about gang behaviour: "members of fashion-conscious youth gangs . . . are now established at virtually every high school in Southern Ontario" (*Globe and Mail,* May 23, 1990:A1, A2); "The flap of the [YOA] act comes at a time when violent youth crime is on the rise and cities are plagued with street gangs" (*Montreal Gazette,* April 8, 1989:B1); and youth gang activity in Ottawa "mirrored a wave of crime committed by youthful gang members that afflicts cities across Canada" (*Maclean's,* May 18, 1992:35). Examples of other types of vague and generic statements about gang-related activity include the use of the word "gang" to refer to small groupings of kids, especially pre-teens: "two gangs of 11-year old grade six students" and "three 10-year old boys physically accosted a nine-year-old and stripped him of his running shoes" (*Maclean's,* May 18, 1992:35).

When youth gang violence occurs, it is undeniably a problem in need of intervention. I do not mean to trivialize the problem. I do wish, though, to suggest that the plague of gang violence is exaggerated and, most importantly, that the images of gang members in the media are based on stereotypes of class, race and family background that both foster and play into already existing stereotypes. In effect, the concept "gang" has become a linguistic referent or code word that fosters powerful visceral reactions against visible minority youth and street kids. Furthermore, when news accounts of gang activity discuss membership, rituals and criminal activity, they either deliberately or inadvertently neglect to discuss: the social and economic reasons why kids congregate in rebellious groups; why affiliation is so important to young people; and the ethical implications of branding all youths who are in groups, especially in public settings like "the mall," as potentially dangerous. When one clears away the ideological smoke and mirrors, it is perfectly understandable that membership in gangs for marginalized and disaffiliated kids—or any kids for that matter—is a simple, collective way to invest their lives with meaning. Notwithstanding the probability that most adults prefer to congregate as well, the unspecific and unbounded use of the word "gang" in media accounts contributes considerably to public panic about kids out of control. One of the most insidious outcomes of such linguistic references is the targeting and scapegoating of visible minorities.

Undoubtedly, the United States is one of the most conspicuously racialized societies in the world, and media factual and fictional accounts of youth crime are, almost without exception, race- and gang-oriented. Because the society is so racialized, it tends to be unreflective and unapologetic about the consequences of discussing youth crime in the context of race. Despite a spate of very fine American movies that attempt to understand the inner city gang and to make gang membership understandable—"The Outsiders," "Boys 'n the Hood" and "Grand Canyon," for example, which I presume should logically have an educative function—mainstream American culture remains alarmingly unreflective about its public portraits of youth crime.

Canada, in contrast, is arguably less racialized than the United States and, although we do not have the inner city race and gang problems that America does, many media accounts of youth gang activity in Canada have a deliberate racial referent. The most obvious example of this is the constant use of gang names, many of which have a racial identifier. Although journalists and editors may argue that it is sound, objective and informative journalism to identify racial groups—and it may help to sell papers—the use of broad categorical linguistic devices such as "Black" or "Asian" or "Native" paints the entire racial category with the same brush and creates an unnecessary, unfounded and generalized crimogenic referent to people of colour.

Media coverage abounds with examples of the use of broad racial terms, including: "police raided the locker of a student at Jarvis Collegiate believed to be a member of the Asian Posse gang" (*Globe and Mail*, May 23, 1990:A1, A2); "two native youths sniggered about their guilty pleas outside the courtroom here before sentencing" (*Saskatoon Star Phoenix,* May 31, 1989:A18); "she was surrounded by 10 Native girls who pushed her to the ground, kicked her and punched her in the face and stole her leather bomber jacket" (*Alberta Report,* July 31, 1995:25). This is a mere sampling of the types of racial referents that occur in media articles. And it is important to consider that racial categories are very general, that they are in some instances subjective and that the identification of race serves no purpose other than to create associations between criminality and race. Consider the following "objective," rather subtly racialized news reports:

> New immigrants, especially Vietnamese, do make up a slightly higher proportion of youth gang members. A few years ago we had the Los Diablos and those Latin gangs in Vancouver. They effectively no longer exist although some Latin people are still involved in criminal activity, but they generally involve gangs of mixed-race composition. (*Vancouver Sun,* February 3, 1994:B1)

> Like all of Canada's major cities, both Edmonton and Calgary have a growing Asian crime problem. In Edmonton, where Vietnamese make up 35% of the Asian population, Vietnamese crime is the biggest threat. (*Alberta Report,* October 26, 1992:22)

> Another so-called gang calls itself the Los Votos Chicanos and is reportedly modelling itself after the Hispanic gangs of East Los Angeles. Police say most youths in the Indian Posse and the Overlords are aboriginal, while the other two gangs are racially mixed. (*Winnipeg Free Press,* September 29, 1994:B1)

A more blatant use of racial references occurs when headlines use excessively large and emboldened print. In these examples, the racial epithet is highly generic and used only with reference to visible minority youth: "The Crooked Credit Card Capital: Calgary Police Blame Surging Fraud on the City's Asian Gangs" (*Alberta Report,* September 21, 1992:22), and "New Insights into Alberta's Asian Crime Scene: The Publicity Angers Edmonton's Viets, But Police Say People Have to Know How Extensive It Is" (*Alberta Report,* October 26, 1992:22). Both headlines attempt to provide readers with a context for reading the articles: youth gang violence is racial, restricted to Asians and well-organized.

Recall the argument I made earlier that these stark and emboldened headlines represent visual clips, much like the visual clips one sees on television, which are short, disconnected and decontextualized and, as a consequence, become embedded on the subconscious, whether or not the viewer continues to read the article. Many consumers of news magazines and newspapers view them in a hurried, cursory manner and these pictures and headlines constitute much of what such readers consume. These stark visual images are ideologically powerful even when presented in the context of a favourable article. Headlines that read "Asian Not Dominant Force in Youth Gangs, New Study Stresses" (*Vancouver Sun,* February 3, 1994:B1) and "The Horror World of 'Mattress Girls': Child Prostitution is Not Unique to Asians, Police Insist" (*Alberta Report,* October 17, 1993:28) represent attempts at even-handed journalism, but the subtle result is that the social problem is once again placed in broad categories of race or ethnic origin. Media accounts never make generic references to white offenders or victims; it would seem ludicrous to the reading public to refer to "white youth offenders" who hang around in groups as "European Canadian gangs," and yet the referent "Asian" is commonplace. Similarly, when the specific country of origin for visible minority youth is known, the country is often mentioned: "the Vietnamese are no strangers to violence" (*Alberta Report,* October 26, 1992:22) and "Vietnamese Are Blamed for Recent Calgary School Violence" (*Alberta Report,* January 2, 1995:28). I would ask the reader to consider the unlikelihood that similar referents to white offenders would appear, suggesting, for example, that the French, English, Austrians or Ukrainians are to blame for youth crime.

The most blatant use of "word-based images" I have encountered in my research was part of a series of articles in the *Winnipeg Free Press* that dealt with the city's burgeoning youth gang problem. One of the articles, a full-page spread, entitled "Angry, Bitter Kids Flex Their Muscles: An Outsider's Guide to Youth Gangs" (*Winnipeg Free Press,* September 29, 1994:B1), contained a pictorial guide to the gangs in Winnipeg with an sketched portrait of a typical gang member and a list of identifiable characteristics, including racial composition, which was either Aboriginal or racially mixed. It is interesting to note that when racial referents are unclear, the term used is "mixed racial" or "racially diverse," never white. This particular article is noteworthy and especially malevolent in its presentation of a poem written by an Indian Posse member to describe the activities and the criminological orientation of Aboriginal youth. The emboldened headline is "Your Racist Blood We Will Spill," and the poem reads:

> The marching feet of the Indian Posse echoes in your mind,
>   getting stronger day by day.
> Our colour is red and its here to stay, some of us have
>   something to prove and some of us already have.
> But all in all we are the Indian Posse and together we stand
>   tall.
> We are a breed that has seen it all and had its better
>   days, but in the end we will learn our true native ways.
> We are warriors and in our mind we will survive the war path.

In the days of old, our people used to fight and kill each
other and, as they did, we will if there is no other way.
We hold our heads high because we are not scared to die for
one another, for we will join the Great Spirit in the sky.
Call us what you will, but it is your racist blood we will
spill.

Brothers Forever: Indian Posse

The use of this essentially pictorial device is noteworthy for several reasons. First, of all the sentiments expressed in the poem, the newspaper chose to use the one inflammatory statement as the headline, despite the fact that the poem contains many other important and socially significant sentiments. Second, the poem is centred in the middle of the page under the large heading "Bad Boys" and, after the primary headline, is the first thing the reader sees. If cursory consumers see only what is stark and highly visible, there is little reason to doubt that they will come away with a sense of fear and disdain for Aboriginal youth.

Racialized presentations are often accompanied by pictures of offenders from a visible minority group. In fact, it is rare to see photographic images of white young offenders. A typical example of such pictorial biases occurred in the *Maclean's* magazine cover story "Kids Who Kill" (Kaihla, DeMont and Wood 1994). The three accounts of youth murders are accompanied by pictures that include victims and their families, crime scenes and, in one case, the offender standing in a prison garden. And this particular offender is quite visibly of Native ancestry. The other two accounts of youth murders, in which the offenders are not Native, do not include visual portraits of the offenders. In case you may be tempted to dismiss this as coincidence, examples of such racialized depictions are common. The article presented earlier (*Western Report* August 31, 1992:25) about three nine-year old boys who were said to "Turn a Town Upside Down and Nobody Can Touch Them" contains a photograph of two obviously Native children described in the caption as "Pre-Criminals Potskin and Trottier." Another typical photographic representation (Figure 4.1) appeared in an article entitled "Youths Treat Crime as a Joke" (*Saskatoon Star Phoenix*, May 31, 1989). The picture and caption identify the youth as Native and incarcerated, ready for release. Similarly, the *Winnipeg Free Press* (October 3, 1994:B2) chose to depict three pictures of youth, all African-American, with the words "Bad Boys . . . All know gunshot victims."

Several observations are important regarding photographic referents. First, photos rarely occur for offenders other than visible minorities. Second, these pictorial depictions serve no journalistic or informational purposes and are, in my opinion, only intended to be inflammatory, partisan and marketable. If this were not the case, depictions of white offenders would be as, or more, numerous

Figure 4.1: *Saskatoon Star-Phoenix* May 31, 1989:A6

than those for visible minorities, given the relative occurrences of youth crime acts.

In general, then, racial references serve both journalistic and ideological purposes. They promote the image of the young offender as unlike the viewer/reader, and in doing so they create identifiability in the stereotype of the young offender. Such images play on already existing racialized biases in the community and use them to create anxiety in the reader. It is alarm that sells, and race-based images of gangs and young offenders predominate in the news because they help sell particular accounts. More distressingly, they help formulate societal opinions and attitudes towards "young folk devils." The use of race as a category of identification—especially when it is done in a consistently selective manner—serves no social purpose other than to create negative associations between racial characteristics and potential dangerousness.

The Ultimate Crime: You Have Chosen to Be Poor

From our discussions to this point, it is obvious that the discourse of news is replete with highly potent words that are codes for stereotypical representations. For example, when news accounts use the word "gang," the latent image is often one of members of visible minorities who live in poor urban areas, and such messages are often accompanied by pictures. Similarly, when depictions of youth crime refer to family disruption, they frequently focus on single mothers or derelict mothers as responsible for youth misconduct. The "family problems" code-phrase indicts the poor parenting of single mothers, decontextualized from economy or society, as the singular cause of youth malevolence.

This last section in this chapter is probably the most important in the book. Here I will argue that the whole culture of criminal representation is based on subtle and embracing messages that the poor are not only responsible for crime but that poverty is crime. The connection between poverty and badness is embedded in the codes of media discourse, and I illustrate how these code words infiltrate what is essentially acceptable vernacular.

In preparing to write this chapter, I decided to study newspaper and news magazines for more than references to young offenders. I observed that the same magazines and newspapers that carried accusatory articles about youth often engaged in poverty bashing, especially targeting those who are dependent on social support. Welfare mothers, indigent and absentee fathers, youths on social support and the able-bodied who collect unemployment insurance all receive public censure through the voices of politicians and right-wing activists who gain access to the public's attention through the news media. The concept of work for welfare, for example, is emblazoned with the ideological message that if people are physically capable of working, then they must either voluntarily or involuntarily be employed. And, of course, this rhetoric is hollow given that many single mothers are fully employed in caring for their families, that laid-off workers have difficulty finding work, especially when economies are stagnating, and that it is not easy for needy citizens to face foodbank line-ups or suffer the scrutiny of the social welfare system. And, not surprisingly, the moral panic against the poor is most vocal and incessant when economies are suffering and when societies face seemingly insurmountable budgetary deficits.

A perfect example of how both being poor and being young get translated into blame is the Saskatchewan NDP government's stance on social assistance and labour. In early 1996, Premier Romanow declared that work for welfare would not be a part of the government's agenda for reducing the deficit, except for adolescents. This particular social democratic government declared, however, that only youths would be singled out for welfare scrutiny under the implication that families should be mandated to care for their adolescents. Similarly, in 1996 the government of British Columbia reduced welfare support to adolescents in favour of mandatory job searches, and Ontario has legislated that sixteen- and seventeen-year-olds on welfare must be under mandatory adult supervision. Although the youths in question are of the age of consent and legally citizens, their youth status and economic needs obviously place them in the path of condemnation. And this, despite evidence put forth by the National Anti-Poverty Organization that the first ones to be hit by downturns in the economy are the young who have a higher unemployment rate (15.2 percent compared to 9.1 percent overall in 1993) than older adults.

My lament is that these policies that attack the young are part of the overall public panic against youth and are likely to drive kids onto the street where they may face exploitation from adults. From an analytical perspective, it is the combination of being young and being poor that surfaces in news media discourse. This excerpt from *Alberta Report* (May 2, 1994:39) is a consummate example:

> Welfare dependency has also contributed to youth crime and family breakdown. Former Alberta crown attorney Scott Newark, now head of the Ottawa-based Canadian Resource Centre for Victims of Crime, argues, "Welfare is not a responsible way of dealing with young people who can just as easily work." It invites trouble by creating a "lifestyle that is fundamentally anti-social. Idleness is not a good thing." Mr. Newark believes that if young males are forced to support themselves, most will find work and the time they have to contemplate criminal behaviour will evaporate.
>
> Sociologists June O'Neill and Anne Hill of Baruch College of the City University of New York seem to have proven this empirically. In their study of inner-city poor, Professors O'Neill and Hill found that the higher the welfare payments, the greater the "negative effects on the behaviour of young men by increasing the likelihood of fathering a child out of wedlock, criminal activity, and by reducing their attachment to the labour force." The duo ultimately concluded that "a 50% increase in the monthly dollar value of welfare benefits led to a 117% increase in the crime rate among young black men."
>
> Such reasoning is, in part, behind Social Services Minister Mike Cardinal's announcement in early April that he wants the 29,000 singles still on welfare in Alberta to be off the rolls by the year 2000.

This excerpt illustrates how absurd the argument is that crime is caused by welfare rather than by poverty, disadvantage, job discrimination, overpolicing and differential access to education. This decontextualized logic, presented as empirically true by two American professors, provides the reader with a neat package that relates welfare, laziness and criminality. As with the Romanow government, this logic applies just to kids and assumes that there is plenty of work if idle youth would simply choose to find a job.

The following examples of the condemnation of poverty are more subtle than the previous example and more circumspect than the attacks on women and mothers, ethnic minorities and "innately evil" adolescents. The first example, taken from the *Calgary Herald,* is curiously a story about a retraction of an obvious attack on mothers and poverty. The article entitled "Moms Furious at MLA's Betrayal: Tory Calls Single Mothers Vindictive Leeches" (*Calgary Herald*, April 18, 1995:A2), describes a verbal attack by an Alberta Member of the Legislative Assembly on single mothers in need who try to collect child support from fathers. The article is based on Premier Ralph Klein's admonition to the MLA that such statements are not appropriate for elected officials. The article goes on to discuss the plight of single mothers, but the majority of the article discusses the unfair burden imposed on divorced fathers by child support. This article is noteworthy for two reasons. First, the headlines contain the condemnatory phrase by the MLA (in bold letters) and if readers go no further, they see the visual connection between single mothers and social leeches. Second, although the article is about the inappropriateness of the comment by the MLA, the premier's condemnation of the statement is dealt with in a very nonchalant manner and then abandoned quickly. Then the rest of the article concentrates on the discrimination suffered by fathers who are required to pay child support.

Although this article contains no references to youth crime, it illustrates an ideology that forms an important basis for news articles that use poverty and motherhood as part of the calculus of crime. Most importantly, it indicates that highly placed individuals can attack, almost with impunity, categories of people who are seen or defined as assailable. Overall, articles on youth crime and its relationship to poverty illustrate, in part, how pervasive and enveloping this ideology against poverty is.

An article in the *Montreal Gazette* (July 18, 1993:C1), entitled "About 30 Kids a Year Charged with Murder," once again illustrates the visceral images created by word connections, in this case, of murder and poverty. The article begins by pointing out that youth murder is a rare event, and the writer acknowledges how the panic over youth murderers is exaggerated. The article then proceeds to discuss several murders and the ensuing "lenient" sentences that were received under the Young Offenders Act. The subtle attack on poor kids comes at the end in a testimonial by a psychologist who suggests that youth murders are so rare that it is difficult to make social or psychological generalizations about young murderers. Most importantly, this discussion is preceded by the suggestion that "[i]f we really care about the poor kids, we should make sure they get the help they need when we send them to correctional facilities," an ostensibly enlightened position. Although the article attempts to be even-handed and progressive, it fuses youth murderers with poor children, a connection that is entirely unsubstantiated. The result is that, while the reader is told to feel some understanding for young murderers, the text clearly generates revulsion and bewilderment and connects their "evil world" with poverty. The final testimonial in the article despairs that "[m]ost kids are subject to impulse, and that often results in something deadly." Again, this alarming statement about the innately dangerous potential of youth (especially poor youth) is patently unsubstantiated but gains credibility as it is voiced by a youth psychologist with a "Dr." in front of his name. This article is typical, then, of accounts that strive for credibility by drawing on the "expert" knowledge of highly placed, highly educated and, by social definition, highly credible individuals.

A similar example that equates murder and poverty appeared previously in this chapter within the statement in the *Calgary Herald* (August 9, 1990:C3) that criminologists and psychologists concur that the families most disposed to produce child killers are headed by the welfare mother and the newly arrived immigrant. This unsubstantiated and false—and, I would add, classist and racist—statement is prefaced with the contention that "while any child can kill, there is a disturbing trend among those who do. They are often abused, neglected and unwanted. Their homes are run more like hotels with parents not bothering if they check in or out." Despite whether this statement is supportable or not, it appears prior to the qualification regarding race and class. This chronology of assertions subtly and unapologetically imputes a connection between welfare, race and "vile parenting."

In other cases, poverty, race and geographical location get mixed together into the code for badness. One article, part of a series of articles dealing with youth gangs which appeared in the *Winnipeg Free Press* (September 29, 1994:B1), presents detailed, graphic and seemingly factual police and court accounts of the nature and composition of gangs and their activities, but embedded within the text is a statement that frames these detailed accounts of gang-based crime. It asserts that the most dangerous gangs are comprised of Aboriginal and racially mixed kids from poor and broken homes in the inner city, and warns that, "with Manitoba leading the nation in child poverty, it's small wonder that the statistics also bear out in higher rates of crime." The connection between poverty and crime (and race and geographical area) is made early and contextualizes the "culture of poverty" explanations that follow, which once again indict the poor, the inner city and racial minorities for creating their own problems. As in most media accounts, social ills are reduced in the final analysis to the individual or the group. Such essentially biological or psychological determinist accounts are sweeping generalizations and at no time reveal that the subcultures they discuss are mostly law-abiding, that most violent and destructive youth crime is committed by only a few youths and that, despite all the disadvantages that a highly stratified society can impose on marginalized groups, these groups create vital communities that, in many instances, are obvious only because they come under society's closest scrutiny. Although statements like those in this article contain some truths, they are most damaging in that they neglect to contextualize crime problems within a social structure in which people are given privilege on the bases of wealth, prestige, race and gender. The real problems that arise when profit takes primacy over individuals are hidden by the "panic of evil children."

Poverty can become the focal point of debates about the origins of crime in an implicit but socially acceptable manner. Such socially acceptable discourse revolves around "family values." For example, an *Alberta Report* (May 2, 1994:38) article, entitled "Two Are Stronger than One: Alberta Teens from

Traditional Families Are Less Drug-Prone," announces that family breakdown is linked to an "explosion of crime, poverty, and drug abuse," and that the dual-parent families more characteristic of affluent society are more effective in preventing teenage drug abuse. Quite clearly, the article contains untruths—asserting that divorce is more common among lower-class people—and illogical assertions—that dual-parent families are stable, safe and nurturing despite evidence to the contrary concerning violence within the nuclear family. Another article (*Western Report*, April 15, 1991:45) quotes a crown attorney who says that "kids in the poorer parts of town where juvenile crime is most common are well aware that in most cases youth court will punish them lightly, if at all—it's just human nature that if you don't get punished you don't worry about doing it again." Once again, the faulty logic that poorer areas are more criminogenic is debatable, in light of a large body of research that suggests that kids in the poorer parts of urban areas do not necessarily commit more crimes than their wealthier counterparts, but that they do get arrested, tried and convicted to greater degrees (Schissel 1993). Once again, the subjective testimonial of a professional spokesperson like a crown attorney is largely undisputed in the eyes of the reading public.

This last example shows how, when the crime in question is a major affront to collective morality, the subtlety and political correctness disappear in favour of protracted and scathing allegations of cultural inferiority. The case is, again, the murder of two-year-old James Bulger. As mentioned the British press went on a rampage of blaming the underclass for the social ills in Britain. Even when cooler heads prevailed, the overwhelming consensus in the British media was that, unless the poor were dealt with, they will continue to be a social and physical threat to traditional British society. An article in the *Winnipeg Free Press* (March 18, 1993:D11) illustrates how this panic emigrated to Canada and was informed by the same type of ideological polemic. Although the article is about England and the ravages that poor economic times can have on a society, it engages in typical media discourse that conceptualizes the underclass as teetering on the verge of a violent social insurrection. This article, entitled "Liverpool, A Tinder-Box," carries a statement by a local port worker that "We're horrified by a murder that can only have been done by the city's underclass, those rotten kids who can and won't work." An additional statement by a probation officer that the "real problem is an underclass developing in this country who have not had experience of work or adequate access to training." The article continues with statements by teachers and police representatives that the problem is simply one of poverty and declining morality: "[W]e've always had a lot of property crime, especially in poor areas in Britain, now we're seeing 13-year-olds who don't see any problem with assaulting people." These rather scathing attacks are endorsed by a statement by the British Social Security Secretary, who is quoted as saying, "No social conditions can excuse a youth from robbing or murdering." By presenting a litany of uncontested statements, the article presents these subjective statements as conclusive facts. The issue of criminogenesis is left to the reader; the basis for judgements is a series of public statements directed against poverty as a vice. By presenting second-hand statements, the editor and writer absolve themselves from responsibility for these unsubstantiated attacks on the underclass while insinuating a sense of plausibility in the claims.

These examples of media discourse against the poor are different in several ways from the invectives against single mothers and racial minorities. Whereas articles against the latter are blatant and generic, media discourse surrounding poverty is much more circumspect and laden with images of the poor as victims of economic circumstance, but all the while it maintains the posture that the poor, as a generic culture, are volatile and potentially criminal. The poor are treated in a much more paternalistic manner than are women and racial minorities; generally, the sentiment is that the poor, while weak in both economy and spirit, need our help. For women and especially racial gangs, the sentiment is much more pointed and castigating, as if women and racial minorities are boldly and deliberately defying society's rules. I would like to add as anecdotal evidence that articles dealing with youth crime and poverty rarely, if ever, use photographs depicting privation. For articles focusing on racialized and feminized crime, photographs of defiant minority gang members or snap-shots of poorly dressed or overweight mothers are commonplace. The reason for the absence of pictorial descriptions of poverty may be that they are too representative of the stratified world, which the average citizen knows about—and may lament—but chooses to ignore.

I have sought in this chapter to show how stereotypes against race, class and gender are embedded in news reports and that much of the information and the visual techniques that support stereotypical presentations lack journalistic integrity. Through selective inclusion of facts, visual manipulation of messages, retraction of blatant inaccuracies, and decontextualization of crime, the news media are distressingly effective and consistent in their presentations of a burgeoning youth crime wave and their condemnations of marginalized people. Even in their most objective moments, the written news media engage in fomenting public alarm over youth and are unreflective and unapologetic about their claims to journalistic integrity. They are the creators of young "folk devils."

Chapter 5

The Reality of Youth Crime and Misconduct

I have titled this chapter partly in irony. The presentations of youth crime we encounter in the media and in political debates are not based on empirical reality but instead on a constructed version that serves political and moral purposes. Of course, my version of the reality for youth could be said to be another interpretation. However, often unsubstantiated and/or inaccurate claims are made in the media against youth. This chapter is an attempt to critique those claims from a perspective that I believe is closely aligned with those of young people.

To this end, I use three different empirical sources to illustrate three kinds of sociological analysis: structural, cultural and personal. My structural analysis is based on Canadian Centre for Justice Statistics data on rates of youth crime over time. Although these trends have been documented recently (Schissel 1993; Statistics Canada 1992), I discuss them in the context of law reform and legal change. Further, I look at changes relative to changes in previous years to get some sense of how official crime rates fluctuate.

The second source of empirical data is a survey of street youth collected by the John Howard Society in Saskatoon in the summer of 1994. The goal of this research was to understand the legal and social lives of marginalized youth. These data give us some sense of the connection between relative privation, social neglect, criminal activity and legal disadvantage.

Third, I use information collected by social services in Saskatoon and Regina on young offenders who had been formally processed by the legal system. This information is based on extensive interviews with the youth as well as supplementary material provided by schools, families and the courts. This wealth of information provides a sense of the personal reality of these "legalized" youth. The data, based on detailed accounts and assessments of the personalities and lives of young offenders, illustrate that many youths who are continually in trouble with the law are victims at a most basic level and became offenders only as a result of their personal, socio-economic and legal victimization. This last set of data is extremely important because it presents the complete and complex reality of the lives of young people, only parts of which we see in news accounts. The parts presented by the media are constructed almost entirely around the criminal act and its legal consequences and rarely around the personal and social circumstances that bring youth into conflict with the law.

Youth Crime Trends and the Politics of Crime Rates

As shown in earlier chapters, there is much misuse of official crime data in news accounts about youth crime and the Young Offenders Act. The overwhelming sentiment is that youth crime rates are exploding and that the leniency of the Young Offenders Act is responsible in part for this epidemic. The Young Offenders Act was passed in Parliament in 1982 to give youth the same rights and freedoms as their adult counterparts. Most importantly, the Act was designed to ensure that accused youth would be adequately represented in court, that their parents or guardians would be informed of their arrest and directed to appear in court, that accused youth would be informed of their rights and every effort would be made to ensure that they are able to make informed decisions about their legal options, and that the names and other references of the accused would be kept in confidence and away from public scrutiny. Most importantly, however, the YOA was passed to ensure that young offenders, whenever possible, would be directed away from the formal legal process and towards alternative measures, including community-based programs of reparation and mediation. In the final analysis, the principles of the YOA were declared to protect the civil liberties of young people in general, and to provide nonjudicial options for young offenders specifically.

If we accept statistics at first blush, as do most news producers, it is clear that there is some reason for concern in light of the temporal changes occurring with the implementation of the YOA. The statistics, like most of the accounts of youth crime, however, are decontextualized. They are presented in a social, economic and political vacuum as if nothing is occurring in society except kids doing bad things. These are really abstracted, pseudo-empirical narratives that present a fictional reality. As we attempt to contextualize national statistics and deconstruct public rhetoric surrounding them, it becomes obvious that youth crime rates are produced by forces other than increasingly evil and dangerous youth.

The data are taken from Statistics Canada and the Canadian Centre for Justice Statistics Uniform Crime Reports (UCR) and are based on "actual incidents," which means only crimes for which individuals are arrested. Furthermore, of all the arrests made, only some proceed to the stage where a charge is laid. Consequently, some youths are not charged but dismissed, generally as a result of the refusal of the victim to lay a charge, diversion strategies or conciliation enforced by the police.

Figures 5.1 and 5.2 show trends for all criminal code offenses committed by youth. Figure 5.1 presents total incidents and the number of incidents handled formally or informally. Remember that the spirit and intent of the Young Offenders Act is to deal informally with young offenders whenever possible.

Figure 5.1. Canadian Youth Criminal Code Offenses: Total, Formal and Informal

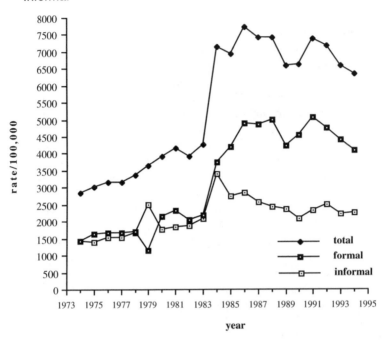

Figure 5.2. Canadian Youth Criminal Code Offenses: Total Charges, Male and Female Charges

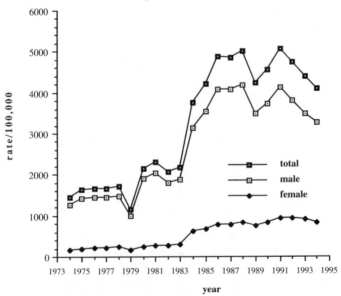

Most notable in the two figures is the rapid increase in official crime rates that occurred after the implementation of the Young Offenders Act in 1983. Much of the initial increase for all youth crime rates can be attributed to the inclusion of seventeen- and eighteen-year-olds in youth court as a result of the Young Offenders Act. An interesting dimension of this state-produced increase is that it contradicts neo-conservative policy regarding less government as better government. In fact, the orthodox conservative reaction to all crimes is, ironically, more state intervention. Despite the political contradictions involved in conservative law-and-order policy, once the YOA had been in place for two years, the increase discontinued and we see evidence of levelling and actual decreases in crime rates, especially from 1990 onward. It is also significant that, in contravention of the philosophy of the YOA, the informal handling of cases— they were not handled by the courts but diverted to community-based agencies—decreased from a peak period in 1984.

Figure 5.2 reillustrates these trends but shows the relative official rates for female and male crimes. In contrast to what we see and hear in the media regarding the "exploding nature" of female crime, the official trends do not show this. In fact, after an initial increase in official rates with the YOA, female crime rates have remained relatively constant.

The next several figures illustrate the trends for specific kinds of youth crime. Figures 5.3 and 5.4 present violent crime rates over time and address one of the major points of contention in public debates about youth crime: that violent youth crime is epidemic.

As with total crime rates, the official rates of violent crimes increased precipitously after the Young Offenders Act began to be enforced. The legacy of the YOA seems to be that crime rates were driven upward, almost in a linear fashion. The only other assumption we can make is that actual violent crime rates were increasing. If this were the case, however, they would not likely coincide so directly with the implementation of the Act. Furthermore, there is mounting evidence that it is precisely the Act and the accompanying public fear of youth that are responsible for increasing violent crime rates. Acts of violence that were previously handled outside of the law—the typical schoolyard fight, for example—are now being formally processed through the courts because people are more likely now than in the past to report acts of youth aggression (Carrington 1995; Gartner and Doob 1994).

What is significant about these figures on violent crimes is that, unlike the trends for overall crimes, they have not receded, except for 1993–94. It is also important that the informal processing of violent cases has not increased proportionately to total incidents rates. In fact, from the 1984 peak period of informal processing, the rates have almost levelled off to the present. Clearly, the police and courts hesitate to implement informal procedures, such as diversion, for crimes of violence, possibly in response to public demands for protection from violent youths. With regard to gender, it appears that the gap

Figure 5.3. Canadian Youth Violent Offenses: Total Incidents, Formal and Informal

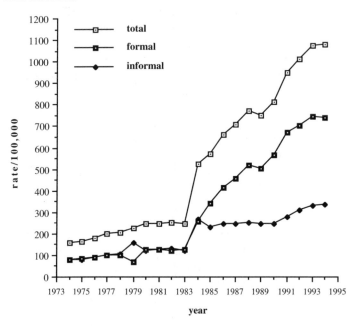

Figure 5.4. Canadian Youth Violent Offenses: Total Charges, Male and Female Charges

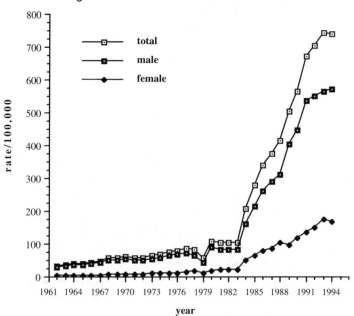

Figure 5.5. Canadian Youth Property Offenses: Total Formal and Informal

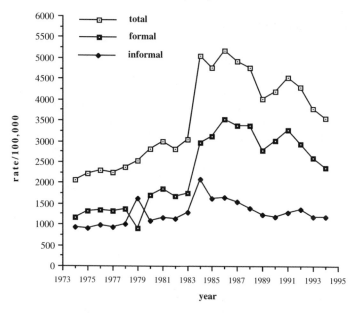

Figure 5.6. Canadian Youth Property Offenses: Total Charges, Male and Female Charges

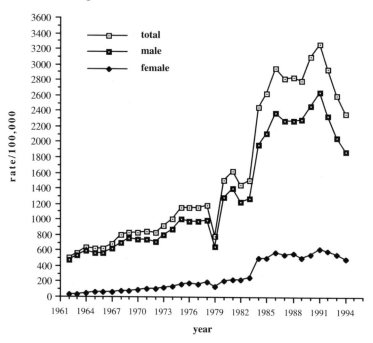

between male and female crime has increased quite dramatically, especially since 1983. These results leave us with little evidence that female youth are becoming more violent relative to their male counterparts or that increases in female youth crime rates are the result of anything but the increased use of legal intervention as a result of the Young Offenders Act.

I include trends for property crimes to show that judicial approaches to youth crime vary depending on the nature and seriousness of crime categories. Much of the public panic over youth crime stresses property damage and the threats to business and property values that youths pose. Figures 5.5 and 5.6 illustrate the trends in total incidents and charges for the generic category of property crimes.

These figures illustrate a dramatic departure in legal trends from the ones presented above. The property crime rates appear to fluctuate quite dramatically from year to year. The marked increases after the YOA are similar to trends for other crimes, but the somewhat erratic fluctuations to 1991 and the rapid decline afterward indicate that police and court practices determine, in large part, official rates of crime. It is improbable that such changes are the result of dramatic fluctuations in crimes committed. Similar to other crime trends for youth, the gap between formal and informal processing has increased to the present, again presenting a paradox to the philosophy and intent of the Young Offenders Act, which was enacted to foster the informal handling of young offender cases.

Figure 5.6 illustrates that youth property crime rates are largely the result of male crime. Although the female rates have increased somewhat, the dramatic increases and decreases are characteristic of male rates. In fact, female youth property crime rates have remained relatively stable since the initial "shock" of the Young Offenders Act. Once again, these trends, especially for male offenders, indicate the volatile nature of youth crime rates.

Figures 5.7 and 5.8 illustrate how the administration of justice affects youth crime rates. The "other" category of crime consists of, particularly for youth, violations of court orders and bail, and violations of the Young Offenders Act such as being at large and failure to appear. Although these are criminal matters, they present very little threat to the public at large and are primarily inconveniences that disrupt the administration of justice. Figures 5.7 and 5.8 show that these crimes that disturb the legal process are dealt with fairly harshly by the courts.

Figure 5.7 illustrates that, like other crimes, the trends rose abruptly after the Young Offenders Act and then tended to level off to the present. Most disconcerting, however, is the trend for informal processing, which increased up to 1985 and then has decreased to the present. Informal processed cases outstripped formal cases up to 1985 and then the relationship reversed. As of 1985, the courts were much less disposed than before to handle cases informally. Once again, it is interesting how the Young Offenders Act precipitated a more

Figure 5.7. Canadian Youth Other Criminal Code Offenses: Total Incidents, Formal and Informal

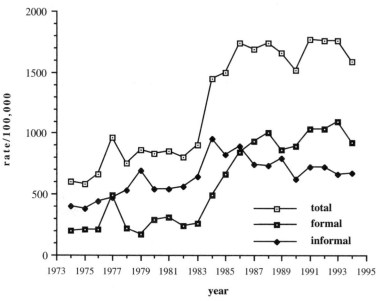

Figure 5.8. Canadian Youth Other Criminal Code Offenses: Total Charges, Male and Female Charges

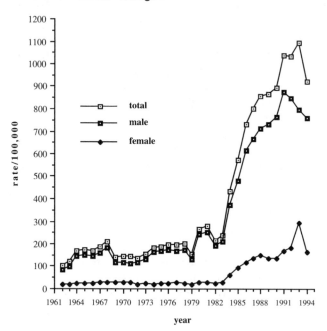

aggressive, punitive approach to youth crimes, especially crimes that do not directly threaten public welfare.

Figures 5.9 and 5.10 contextualize trends of increasing youth crime rates. They compare youth crime rates to adult crime rates, and the trend lines are based on ratios of youth rates to overall crime rates for total incidents and charges. The ratios indicate the prevalence of youth crime rates relative to overall crime rates. For example, a ratio of 0.1 would indicate that the overall crime rate is ten times the youth crime rate, or that for every one youth crime on the books, there are ten adult crimes.

Figure 5.9 illustrates that total criminal code violation incident rates for youth compared to adults rose quite sharply, but once again only as a result of the Young Offenders Act. In fact, after the initial impact of the Act, the ratio of youth crime to adult crime became quite level. For total charges, the same phenomenon exists, with a rapid increase in charges for youth relative to adults and then a complete levelling off. It is especially significant that the YOA widened the gap between the ratios for total incidents and charges, indicating that, relative to adults, youth are dealt with more formally now than before 1983, and increasingly more formally relative to adults. As stated before, the opposite was supposed to have happened in light of the Young Offenders Act, which was struck to deal informally with youths whenever possible.

Figure 5.10 illustrates the same ratios as Figure 5.9 for crimes of violence. The patterns here are substantially unlike those for all criminal code violations. Clearly, the official rates of total incidents and charges have increased for youths relative to the entire population. One of the contentions of conservative ideologues is that violent youth crime is epidemic. It is important, though, to consider that much of the increase in youth violent crime is the result of the increased tendency of police and courts to deal formally with young offenders. This consideration is evidenced in Figure 5.10 by the intersecting trend lines. Up to the 1983 YOA, the ratios for total incidents and charges were consistently similar, indicating that the court's orientation towards adults and youths was similar with regard to the use of formal justice. After 1983, however, the ratio of youth to adult charges rose more abruptly than the ratios for total incidents. The changes in trend lines after 1983 indicate quite clearly that the formal letter of the law was applied more rigidly to youth than to adults. While total incidents remained relatively stable with just a slight increase after 1983, the charges for youths relative to adults rose considerably. It is clear from this graph and previous findings in this chapter that much of the reality of post-YOA youth crime involves the increasing use of formal law to deal with young offenders as a group and in comparison to adults.

Overall, the trend lines for youth crime rates illustrate several phenomena that are rarely mentioned in public and political accounts of youth crime. That the Young Offenders Act drove up crime rates is irrefutable. The Act created a new orientation towards arrest and court processing that was more formalistic

Figure 5.9. Ratio Young Offenders to all Offenders, All Criminal Code Violations

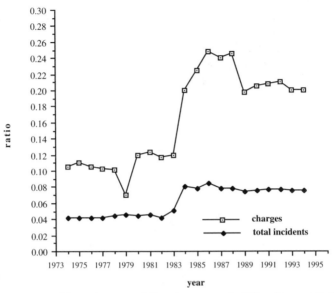

Figure 5.10. Ratio Young Offenders to all Offenders, All Crimes of Violence

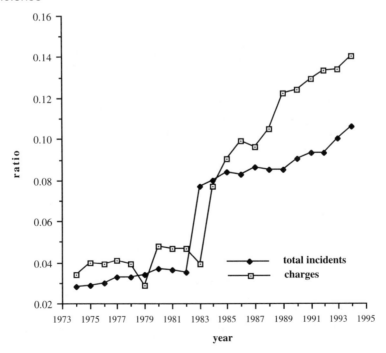

and, I would argue, more punitive. Second, with regard to general crime rates, there is no reason to assume that youths are more criminal than before, especially when we observe declining crime rates in the last five years. Also, when we compare youth crime rates to adult rates, there is little evidence to support the contention that youth are progressively more dangerous. The major conclusion from adult-youth comparisons is that youths are being dealt with increasingly more harshly than adults. Last, when we observe the trends for specific crimes, it is evident that much of the increase in youth crime rates is the result of violations of court rulings and not, as public sentiment would suggest, largely the result of threats to person and property.

The Culture of Youth in Trouble

In the summer of 1994, the John Howard Society in Saskatoon conducted a interview survey of street youth in the city. One hundred and seventy-nine youth were contacted through various social agencies and drop-in centres and were asked to answer a questionnaire regarding their socio-economic background, familial experiences and experiences with the legal system. Some of the results of this project are presented here to illustrate how social characteristics have an impact on the nature and extent of youth contacts with the legal system. This is essentially an empirical study of a subculture of marginalized and disadvantaged youth who live, at least part-time, on the street. They are not necessarily distinguishable by their criminality, their socio-economic background or their appearance. They are distinguishable by their geographic position and their social visibility.

The data are presented in tables and broken down by race, class (where possible) and gender. By presenting the data in this way, I hope to illustrate the influences that social characteristics have on disadvantage. I have argued in previous chapters that criminal/moral stigma has become enmeshed with certain social groups through the discourse of crime news; the following analysis is intended to illustrate how such traits determine life chances. In essence, I show that youth who receive society's venom in the media receive the same type of censure in everyday life.

Race, Class, Gender and Legality

Table 5.1 illustrates arrests of street youth on the bases of gender, race and wealth. This table presents one of the most telling visions of the world of street youth.

Youth crime is rather widespread and spans all class and geographic areas. A number of studies have suggested that youth crime spans social class, race and geography, but that the differential crime rates for these areas are indicative of the differential application of justice, especially differential policing (Schissel 1993; Elliot and Ageton 1980; LeBlanc 1983). Youths who occupy the downtown core of any city are visible by their presence on the street, often by their

Table 5.1. Arrests of Street Youth by Background

Arrest Type		Gender		Race		Wealth			Total
		m	f	Abor	non-Ab	low	med	high	
Arrested	yes	64.4	52.7	*77.0*	*44.2*	*63.6*	*44.2*	*63.6*	59.1
(N=164)	no	35.6	47.3	*23.0*	*55.8*	*36.4*	*55.8*	*36.7*	40.9
Arrested	yes	8.7	7.9	*3.6*	*14.7*	11.1	4.3	10.5	8.3
Drugs	no	91.4	92.1	*96.4*	*85.3*	88.9	95.7	89.5	91.7
Arrested	yes	*32.8*	*57.9*	*35.7*	*52.9*	*29.6*	*60.9*	*44.7*	42.7
Shoplifting	no	*67.2*	*42.1*	*64.3*	*47.1*	*70.4*	*39.1*	*55.3*	57.3
Arrested	yes	25.9	15.8	19.6	20.6	14.8	21.7	26.3	21.9
Assault	no	74.1	84.2	80.4	79.4	85.2	78.3	73.7	78.1
Arrested	yes	*36.2*	*15.8*	*33.9*	*17.6*	*22.2*	*8.7*	*42.1*	28.1
Break/Enter	no	*63.8*	*84.2*	*66.1*	*82.4*	*77.8*	*91.3*	*57.9*	71.9
Arrested	yes	*27.6*	*5.3*	21.4	17.6	25.9	13.0	15.8	18.8
Mischief	no	*72.4*	*94.7*	78.6	82.4	74.1	87.0	84.2	81.2
Arrested	yes	*32.8*	*5.3*	23.2	20.6	33.3	13.0	18.4	21.9
Theft	no	*76.2*	*94.7*	76.8	79.4	66.7	87.0	81.6	78.1
Reoffended	yes	*77.6*	*53.0*	*74.5*	*58.8*	*60.7*	*54.5*	*81.1*	68.8
	no	*22.4*	*47.0*	*25.5*	*41.2*	*39.3*	*45.5*	*18.9*	31.2
Breach of	yes	*50.0*	*30.6*	*50.9*	*25.0*	*32.1*	*20.0*	*61.1*	42.4
YOA/Court	no	*50.0*	*69.4*	*49.1*	*75.0*	*67.9*	*80.0*	*38.9*	57.6

Note: Statistically significant results in italics. All numbers are percentages. Wealth is explained in text. N=96 for all categories except "arrested."

ethnic identity and, as a result of pressure from the business community, are likely to experience the continued surveillance of the police.

For example, Table 5.1 indicates that 59.1 percent of street youth have been arrested at one time or another, considerably higher than for youths in more suburban areas of the city. Furthermore, Aboriginal youths are arrested more (77 percent) than non-Aboriginal youth (44.2 percent), and males are arrested more than females, although the differences between males and females are neither substantial nor statistically significant. Given the cutoff points, it appears that the poorest and wealthiest of street youths are arrested most often, and that youth of average income are the most immune from arrest. This result, however, must be situated in the definitions of wealthy and poor; a family income of $25,000 is not at all high, but it is the cutoff point for the most wealthy street youth.

Despite this, the relationship between wealth and arrests is interesting. For the average non-street young person, greater wealth generally protects against legal involvement (Schissel 1993; West 1991; Reid-MacNevin 1991; Chambliss 1969), but obviously this is not necessarily the case for street youth.

Table 5.1 also shows how arrests for different offenses are related to social categories. For example, for all the crime-specific arrest categories except shoplifting, arrests for males are relatively higher than for females, especially for offenses such as theft and mischief. This phenomenon suggests two things: that males likely engage in more offenses than females (with the exception of shoplifting), and that males are more closely watched by the police and more likely to be arrested instead of warned. Remember, as well, that this close legal scrutiny is much more common for all these youth than for the average youth in society.

Race has an impact on all categories of arrest except for violence, mischief and theft. This finding is consistent with past research that suggests that Aboriginal peoples are watched more closely by the police than their non-Aboriginal counterparts, especially for minor offenses (Hamilton and Sinclair 1991; LaPrairie 1988). The two exceptions here are arrests for drug use and shoplifting; for these two violations, non-Aboriginal youth are more susceptible to arrest. In addition, it is important to emphasize that Aboriginal youth experience the highest relative occurrences of arrest for breaches of the YOA and breaches of court orders, relatively innocuous and harmless offenses—an indication that possibly racial prejudice and stereotypical thinking by the courts disadvantage Aboriginal kids, especially for inoffensive violations.

Finally, Table 5.1 reveals that wealth has a definite impact on arrests for specific crimes and, as shown previously, higher levels of wealth do not necessarily protect street youth from arrest. In fact, for the more aggressive crimes such as assault and break and enter, higher income youths are arrested more often than those with moderate and lower family incomes. Furthermore, the poorest of street youth seem to be arrested only for mischief and theft more than their wealthier counterparts.

Overall, the results indicate the importance of viewing youth crime as partly produced by the police and the justice system, and as directed differentially to the disadvantage of some groups. With the exception of shoplifting, arrests for conventional crimes are relatively low, especially for drug use. However, the system-generated offenses (breach of YOA/court) are quite high, and this is partly what we see in the increases in youth crime after the implementation of the YOA. Importantly, it appears that street kids are often arrested, but mostly for YOA-related offenses and not for drug and violent offenses, as the media would have us believe. The results of this study clearly show that the violence and drug abuse by street kids that are so often posed in the press as threatening to the average citizen are simply untrue. What is evident, however, is that these same villainized kids are substantially victimized by the conditions and the bureaucratic rigidity of the Young Offenders Act.

Furthermore, reoffending rates are quite high; the rates are higher for males than females, for Aboriginal youth than non-Aboriginal, and for more wealthy youth than their poorer counterparts. Most importantly, the overall reoffending rate is 68.8 percent, and high recidivism rates remain a principal reason why right-wing law-and-order advocates attack the rehabilitation-based, curative model of justice. A possible response to the "we told you so" critics of the Young Offenders Act is that street youth remain on the margins of society after their first offense. It is understandable, therefore, that their offending activity will persist and that the close scrutiny by the police will also persist. The justice system, in reacting to the initial offense, is unable or unwilling to address the socio-economic context in which street youth live, so re-arrest is highly likely. Table 5.1 illustrates that street life is really a glass bubble under which highly visible, probably highly defiant and marginalized kids live. The day-to-day reality of their lives may be one of higher incidents of misconduct compared to all youth (my research and that of others would show that it is not considerably higher) and certainly of closer surveillance by the law (Schissel 1993; West 1984). If most youth were under the same level of surveillance as street youth, their recorded offending behaviour—if not arrests—would be as high. I would suggest that the life of the typical street youth is a combination of legal and socio-economic oppression.

Race, Class, Gender and Legal Victimization

One of the fundamental tenets of the Young Offenders Act is that each youth offender should not only have access to legal representation but should actually have legal representation present in court. Furthermore, youth are to be accompanied by parents or guardians and they are to be fully aware of their legal rights and privileges. Like their adult counterparts, youths are to experience fair and equal legal treatment as mandated by the Young Offenders Act and the Charter of Rights and Freedoms. Table 5.2 addresses whether these fundamental human rights accrue to street youth and, if not, on what bases legal rights are denied.

Most noticeably, street youths are not consistently represented by counsel. Only slightly more than half have counsel in court. This phenomenon, which contravenes the YOA, is more pronounced for males than females: only 43.2 percent of males had legal representation, compared to 62.5 percent of females. Aboriginal youths have greater levels of legal representation than non-Aboriginals, although the relationship is weak and nonsignificant. As might be expected, the wealthiest street youths have the greatest access to legal counsel, especially over youth in the medium-income range.

Street youths are not always accompanied by parents or guardians in court: only 75.7 percent of the time overall. Class appears to have no bearing on the degree of parental presence, but race does. Interestingly, Aboriginal youth are accompanied 80 percent of the time, compared to non-Aboriginal youth at 63.6

Table 5.2. Legal Rights Protection for Street Youth by Background

Legal Right		Gender		Race		Wealth			Total
		f	m	Abor	non-Ab	low	med	high	
Lawyer	yes	*62.5*	*43.2*	56.4	45.5	50.0	39.1	61.1	54.8
	no	*37.5*	*56.8*	43.6	54.5	50.0	60.9	38.9	45.2
Parents/	yes	80.4	68.4	*80.0*	*63.6*	74.1	78.3	72.2	75.7
Guardian	no	19.6	31.6	*20.0*	*36.4*	25.9	21.7	27.8	24.3
Aware of	yes	87.5	94.6	90.7	91.2	92.6	86.4	88.9	90.3
Right to	no	12.5	5.4	9.3	8.8	7.4	13.6	11.1	9.7
Lawyer									
Aware of	yes	76.2	82.8	80.0	75.0	80.0	89.5	70.4	78.9
Court	no	23.8	17.2	20.0	25.0	20.0	10.5	29.6	21.1
Proceedings									
Fair Treat-	yes	81.5	87.9	86.8	78.6	*87.5*	*100.0*	*80.6*	83.9
ment in	no	18.5	12.1	13.2	21.4	*12.5*	—	*19.4*	16.1
Court									
Lawyer for	yes	*58.7*	*41.9*	52.2	48.0	54.5	50.0	48.4	51.9
Reoffense	no	*41.3*	*58.1*	47.8	52.0	45.5	50.0	51.6	48.1

Note: Statistically significant results in italics. N=97.

percent. Possibly, this reflects initiatives by Aboriginal communities and tribal councils to provide family or community support to young offenders in the form of Native counselling services. Finally, female youth are accompanied by parents or guardians more than males.

In terms of awareness of legal rights and proceedings, most street youth seem relatively aware of the justice system, and there are no differences across categories of race, class and gender. It is significant, though, that approximately 20 percent of street youth who have been in court are still not aware of court proceedings and roughly 10 percent of youth who have been in court are still not aware of their right to legal counsel.

Table 5.3 is based on a sample of eighty-six youths who received sentences through youth court. One of the tenets of the Young Offenders Act is that youth, whenever possible, should receive dispositions that are alternatives to custody. Community service and restitution are programs that reflect the anticustodial sentiment of the YOA. That the highest proportions of sentences are community service (36 percent), mediation (24 percent) and probation (44.7 percent) is evidence that the YOA is being applied in part. However, disparities across groups illustrate the preferential nature of justice as applied to youth. The greatest disparities appear in the open custody category: males receive open custody more than females, Aboriginal youth more than non-Aboriginal, and youths from wealthier families more than from poorer families. As for closed custody, the only disparity occurs for race: Aboriginal youth receive closed custody significantly more often than non-Aboriginal youth. The other two results worthy of discussion are that males receive probation more than females, and non-Aboriginal youth receive mediation more than Aboriginal youth.

The results on sentencing, much like the results on arrests and legal rights, illustrate again that social designations such as race, gender and wealth influence justice to the disadvantage of marginal categories of youth. Tables 5.1–5.3 illustrate that street youth are policed heavily, often experience justice in the absence of knowledge of legal rights and proceedings, and receive sentences based partly on their social characteristics. This last point is significant because it supports findings that street youth are more likely to experience prejudicial justice when their legal rights are abrogated. The absence of legal protection is likely to result in greater levels of discriminatory sentencing, and this appears to be the reality for street youth.

Table 5.3. Sentences of Street Youth by Background

Sentence Type		Gender		Race		Wealth			Total
		m	f	Abor	non-Ab	low	med	high	
Community	yes	40.0	30.6	32.7	35.5	33.3	33.3	39.4	36.0
Service	no	60.0	69.4	67.3	64.5	66.7	66.7	60.6	64.0
Mediation	yes	22.0	28.6	*18.8*	*35.5*	21.7	28.6	30.3	24.7
	no	87.0	71.4	*81.2*	*64.5*	78.3	71.4	69.7	75.3
Open	yes	*16.0*	*2.9*	12.5	6.5	*8.8*	—	*18.2*	10.6
Custody	no	*84.0*	*97.1*	87.5	93.5	*91.3*	*100.0*	*81.8*	89.4
Closed	yes	12.0	5.7	*12.5*	*3.2*	8.7	—	12.1	9.4
Custody	no	88.0	94.3	*87.5*	*96.8*	91.3	100.0	87.9	90.6
Restitution	yes	6.0	5.7	6.3	6.5	—	9.5	9.1	5.9
	no	94.0	94.3	93.7	93.5	100.0	90.5	90.9	94.1
Probation	yes	*56.0*	*28.6*	50.0	35.5	43.5	28.6	51.5	44.7
	no	*44.0*	*71.4*	50.0	64.5	56.5	71.4	48.5	55.3
Fine	yes	12.0	17.1	12.5	16.1	21.7	14.3	6.1	14.1
	no	88.0	82.0	87.5	83.9	78.3	85.7	93.9	85.9

Note: Statistically significant results in italics. N=86.

Race, Class, Gender and Social Injury

Table 5.4 gives us a sense of the social and personal lives of street youth and some insights into why adolescents end up living on the street. The variables include indicators of social and familial treatment and attributes associated with privilege, including education, family and security. This important series of descriptors illustrates the absence of privilege and the presence of victimization for street youth relative to youths located in more privileged sectors of society.

First, many of the youths on the street have run away from home, and this reality is more pronounced for females than males, for Aboriginal youths than non-Aboriginal and for the lowest and highest categories of family wealth. Furthermore, running away appears to be a serious, pre-meditated action—not the type of whimsical activity that all youths at one time or another threaten because many youths run away for periods of longer than one month (41.2 percent). It is interesting that while girls run away more than boys, they stay away for shorter periods.

Second, the treatment youths receive on the street is indicative of their marginality: 57.5 percent of youth indicate maltreatment at the hands of the police. Slightly higher levels of poor treatment are reported by males, Aboriginals and the poorest youth. Furthermore, of the eighty-one youths who reported abusive treatment by the police, 42 percent reported harassment and 22.2 percent reported physical abuse. These are types of police demeanour that would certainly not be tolerated in more privileged sectors of society. While police harassment occurs less for Aboriginal youths than non-Aboriginal youths, physical abuse levels are much higher for Aboriginal youths (34.2 percent versus 10.5 percent). It is also noteworthy that male and female youth are similarly physically abused, but females are harassed by the police less than males.

If we read down Table 5.4 to treatment in custodial institutions, it appears that as a rule such institutions treat youths in custody quite well (88.6 percent) and that treatment does not depend on social categories. The only noticeable exception to this is that males seem to be treated better than females (91.3 percent versus 83.3 percent). The same results appear for staff support within institutions. Generally, it appears that youths suffer poor treatment by the legal system on the street much more than in institutions.

Turning to treatment in familial situations, it is quite evident that the lives of street youth are characterized by abuse at many levels. Fifty of the 179 youths interviewed in this project reported abuse at home and 56 percent of these reported multiple abuse, including physical and sexual. Interestingly, race, wealth and gender appear to have little significant influence on abuse. Furthermore, of the fifty-five youths who had spent time in foster homes, 37.7 percent reported abuse, and again the abuse seems to occur despite gender, race or wealth. Last, 40.4 percent of the youth interviewed had parents who had been convicted of a crime, and this reality is most pronounced for Aboriginal and wealthier youth.

Table 5.4. Life Experiences for Street Youth by Background

Experience		Gender		Race		Wealth			Total
		m	f	Abor	non-Ab	low	med	high	
Runaway	yes	*41.9*	*60.5*	*62.7*	*36.7*	*53.3*	*33.3*	*60.7*	50.3
From Home	no	*58.1*	*39.5*	*37.3*	*63.3*	*46.7*	*66.7*	*39.3*	49.7
N=169									
Length of	month+	*56.4*	*28.3*	38.3	44.8	45.8	22.2	37.8	41.2
Runaway	month-	*43.6*	*71.7*	61.7	55.2	54.2	77.8	62.2	58.8
N=85									
Police	bad	*64.4*	*49.3*	61.4	55.8	67.4	49.0	56.9	57.5
Treatment	good	*35.6*	*50.7*	38.6	44.2	32.6	51.0	43.1	42.5
N=169									
Police	harassment	46.9	34.4	*34.2*	*44.7*	48.0	36.4	48.3	42.0
Treatment	phys.abuse	22.4	21.9	*34.2*	*10.5*	4.0	27.3	17.2	22.2
Type	lack respect	12.1	31.3	*10.5*	*31.6*	28.0	27.3	17.2	19.8
N=81	racism	4.1	3.1	*7.9*	-	8.0	-	-	3.7
	intimidate	14.3	9.4	*13.2*	*13.2*	12.0	9.1	17.2	12.3
Home Abuse	physical	15.4	8.3	11.8	15.4	30.0	-	10.3	12.0
N=50	mental	20.8	12.5	20.6	30.8	10.0	37.5	24.1	22.0
	sexual	7.7	12.5	11.8	7.7	10.0	12.5	10.3	10.0
	multiple	46.2	66.7	55.9	46.2	50.0	50.0	55.2	56.0
Foster Home	yes	38.5	33.3	40.6	25.0	41.7	18.2	42.3	37.7
Abuse	no	61.5	66.7	59.4	75.0	58.3	81.8	57.7	62.3
N=53									
Treatment	poor	8.7	16.7	11.2	16.7	-	16.7	11.1	11.4
in Custody	good	91.3	83.3	88.9	83.3	100.0	83.3	88.9	88.6
N=33									
Staff	nonsupport	21.7	18.2	19.2	33.3	-	33.3	23.5	20.6
Support	supportive	78.3	81.8	80.8	66.7	-	66.7	76.5	79.4
N=33									
Employment	full-time	12.5	13.3	*4.2*	*20.5*	*11.6*	*17.6*	*5.2*	12.9
Status	part-time	13.6	18.7	*8.3*	*19.2*	*30.2*	*19.6*	*3.4*	16.0
N=163	none	73.9	68.0	*87.5*	*60.3*	*58.1*	*62.7*	*91.4*	71.2
School	yes	71.4	80.3	70.3	79.7	*84.1*	*90.6*	*65.0*	75.4
N=167	no	28.6	19.7	29.7	20.3	*15.9*	*9.4*	*35.0*	24.6
Family	both parents	29.3	23.7	*9.5*	*45.6*	*21.4*	*56.6*	*4.9*	26.9
Status	mother	23.9	19.7	*27.0*	*15.2*	*31.0*	*1.9*	*34.4*	22.0
N=168	blended	9.8	19.7	*16.2*	*12.7*	*7.1*	*18.9*	*16.4*	14.7
	foster	2.2	3.9	*2.7*	*1.3*	*4.8*	*3.8*	*1.6*	3.0
	relatives	7.6	6.6	*9.5*	*6.3*	*11.9*	*7.5*	*3.3*	7.1
	alone	14.1	15.8	*14.9*	*15.2*	*14.3*	*3.8*	*24.6*	14.9
	friends	13.1	10.5	*20.3*	*3.8*	*9.5*	*7.6*	*14.8*	11.9

Foster Home	yes	26.1	32.0	*46.7*	*8.0*	*20.5*	*15.7*	*50.0*	28.8
N=155	no	73.9	68.0	*53.3*	*92.0*	*79.5*	*84.3*	*50.0*	71.2
Parents/	yes	34.4	47.4	*58.1*	*26.9*	*39.5*	*27.8*	*54.1*	40.4
Guardian	no	65.6	52.6	*41.9*	*73.1*	*60.5*	*72.2*	*45.9*	59.6
CrimeN=166									
Prostitution	yes	*10.7*	24.3	21.8	6.1	7.4	*4.8*	26.3	16.1
N=93	no	*89.3*	75.7	78.2	93.9	92.6	*95.8*	73.7	83.9
Arrested	yes	58.9	56.8	*63.6*	*43.8*	*61.5*	*38.1*	*67.6*	58.1
while Drunk	no	41.1	43.2	*36.4*	*56.3*	*38.5*	*61.9*	*32.4*	41.9
/DrugsN=93									
Friends	yes	*85.9*	*96.0*	94.5	86.1	86.7	85.2	96.7	90.4
Arrested	no	*14.1*	*4.0*	5.5	13.9	13.3	14.8	3.3	9.6
N=167									

Note: Statistically significant results in italics.

The last set of variables gives some idea of the social nature of street youth. For example, 26.9 percent of the youth who were interviewed came from traditional two-parent families, 14.7 percent from blended (remarried spouses) families, and 7 percent lived with relatives. Almost 50 percent of street youth come from what society would consider conventional extended or nuclear families. Contrary to media stereotypes of criminogenic families, only 22 percent were raised by single mothers. Finally, and very telling, more than 25 percent of street youth either live alone or with friends and consequently do not have access to family support of any type, further evidenced by the reality that 28.8 percent of all street youth interviewed had lived in a foster home. The reality of family displacement is more pronounced for Aboriginal youth: 35 percent were living alone or with friends, and 46.7 percent had lived in foster homes.

In terms of economic and social survival, 75.4 percent of street youths were in school, contrary to popular belief, and 71.2 percent were unemployed. The unemployment problem for youth is most pronounced for Aboriginal youth (only 4.2 percent of whom are employed full-time) and wealthier youth (5.2 percent employed). Distressingly, 16.1 percent of street youth survive by engaging in prostitution. The degree of involvement in prostitution is relatively high if the youth is female (although 10.7 percent of males have prostituted themselves), Aboriginal (21.8 percent) or comes from a relatively wealthy family (26.3 percent). Finally, the vast majority of street youth associate with others who have been involved with the law. The variable "friends arrested" clearly indicates that the street youth peer group is characterized by confronta- tions with the law. It is significant, in this regard, that many of the arrests that occur among street youth occur while under the influence of alcohol, a phenomenon most evident if the youth is Aboriginal or from the poorest or wealthiest families.

The moral panic caused by media depictions of youth crime have been based on he presumptions that youth are evil and out of control, come from certain segments of society and victimize or are a potential threat to the average citizen. When we consider the foregoing profile of youth on the street, it is absurd to discuss the vileness of youth crime. These youth undoubtedly break the law, but so do youth from all geographic and socio-economic categories. Furthermore, the legal rights of street youth are often violated both on the street and in court, and one could easily argue that they are victims of social and legal injustice. In addition, many youths are disaffiliated from conventional familial supports and are essentially on their own. This is compounded by a labour market that hesitates to employ youth and exploits them when they are employed. Lastly, many of the factors that place street youth at risk, such as prescription drugs and alcohol, prostitution and abuse in domestic situations, are adult creations, but the responsibility for the exploitive effects of such adult indulgences are usually placed on "the culture of bad youth."

A Profile of Legalized Youth

The information presented in this section was gathered from social services records on young offenders in Saskatoon and Regina over a six-month period. The profiles consisted of professional assessments of youths, family and social characteristics and judicial information. The data give us some sense of the diversity of young people who run afoul of the law. While the previous section dealt with a group of street youth, this section presents a psychological and social snapshot of the young offender who becomes a legalized subject through contact with the courts. Therefore we are dealing with kids from various socio-economic contexts and not just kids on the street. The following tables show what media accounts and public perceptions ignore: that most youths in contact with the law—not necessarily youths who commit crimes, but youths who are detected—have suffered inordinate personal and social victimization prior to offending, and that this victimization has a substantial impact on their life chances and legal experiences. It is important to remember that the Young Offenders Act was struck in the spirit of recognizing that offending children are victims as well as offenders, but public sentiment and political will are ignorant of this fact or have chosen to ignore it.

Personality Problems and Family Life

Table 5.5 illustrates the types of personality problems that legalized youth experience related to the problems their parents experienced. Statistically significant associations (in this case represented by percentages) are indicated by bold type.

First, it is significant that parental psychiatric problems, identified as either mother or father under psychiatric care, contribute to offspring behavioural problems, verbal aggression and physical aggression against others. In fact, for all three relationships, the differences in percentages are quite large (for the category of "often," approximately 40 percent), suggesting that parental psychiatric trauma predisposes children to certain personality problems, which predispose them to legal involvement. The same conclusions can be drawn for substance abuse, although drug and alcohol abuse seem to create more types of personality problems than do parental psychiatric problems. For example, parental alcohol abuse affects all of the personality problems, rendering children of alcoholic parents relatively likely to be aggressive verbally and physically (towards persons and property), to be angrier, to withdraw, to seek attention and to display defensive behaviour and general behavioural problems. The effects of parental drug abuse are similar, although not as pronounced for defensive behaviour and physical aggression. Last, marital discord affects most of the personality problems that young offenders experience, with the exception of general behavioural problems and physical aggression towards property.

One of the anomalies in Table 5.5 is that, with the exception of parental alcohol abuse, none of the parental problems affects physical aggression towards property; and, for alcohol abuse, the percentage differences across categories are relatively small. We receive some indication here that offenses involving property destruction are the result of influences that most likely do not involve parental problems. More important, however, are the effects that parental problems have on other types of aggressive behaviour, especially anger, physical aggression towards others and verbal aggression.

Table 5.6 continues this analysis by assessing the effects that childhood abuse has on consequent personality problems for convicted young offenders. At first glance, it is indeed significant and startling that, with one exception, all of the relationships between abuse and personality problems are significant. High levels of all types of abuse lead to high levels of personality problems. Furthermore, in most of the relationships, the percentage differences across categories are quite high (indicative of relatively strong relationships), especially when comparing the extreme categories of problems, "none" and "often." For example, for the relationship between physical abuse and anger, the percentage difference between "none" and "often" for "no anger" is 37 percent and for "often anger" is 54.6 percent.

Quite clearly, this table illustrates that all types of abuse have significant traumatic effects on children's abilities to cope and constrain themselves. Furthermore, the previous table illustrates that parental trauma also contributes to children's social and personal disabilities.

Personal Problems and Family Life

Tables 5.7 and 5.8 further this analysis by assessing the impact that parental problems and childhood abuse have on personal problems. Table 5.7 relates parental psychiatric problems, substance abuse and marital problems to the

Table 5.5: Youth Problems with Life Skills by Parental Problems

Youth Problems		Psychiatric		Alcohol		Drugs		Marital Discord		Total
		yes	no	yes	no	yes	no	yes	no	
Behavioural Problems	none	-	4.9	-	8.0	3.6	4.8	-	5.6	5.3
	some	12.5	52.8	38.5	61.4	25.0	57.6	37.5	53.6	50.7
	often	87.5	42.4	61.5	30.7	71.4	37.6	62.5	40.8	44.1
Passivity/ Withdrawal	none	12.4	49.3	29.7	60.2	25.0	52.0	20.8	52.0	47.4
	some	62.6	40.3	51.6	34.1	50.0	39.8	54.2	40.0	41.4
	often	25.0	10.4	18.8	5.7	25.0	8.2	25.0	8.0	11.2
Defensive Behaviour	none	-	32.6	17.2	40.9	21.4	33.1	8.3	35.2	30.9
	some	62.5	44.4	51.6	40.9	50.0	44.4	54.2	44.8	45.4
	often	37.5	23.0	31.3	18.2	28.6	22.6	37.5	20.0	23.7
Verbal Aggression	none	-	40.3	23.4	47.4	17.9	42.7	12.5	44.0	37.5
	some	37.5	43.8	50.0	38.6	64.3	37.9	62.5	39.2	43.4
	often	62.5	16.0	26.6	13.6	17.9	19.4	25.0	16.8	19.1
Physical Aggression (others)	none	-	36.1	21.9	42.0	14.3	38.7	12.5	37.6	33.6
	some	37.5	41.0	40.6	42.0	46.4	40.3	41.7	41.6	41.4
	often	62.5	22.9	37.5	15.9	39.3	21.0	45.8	20.8	25.0
Physical Aggression (property)	none	-	31.3	18.8	36.4	14.3	32.8	16.7	32.0	28.9
	some	75.0	57.6	62.5	56.8	71.4	56.0	58.3	58.4	59.2
	often	25.0	11.1	18.8	6.8	14.3	11.2	25.0	9.6	11.8
Anger	none	-	33.3	15.6	43.2	14.3	35.5	12.5	35.2	31.6
	some	12.5	20.8	21.9	18.2	17.9	21.0	12.5	22.4	19.7
	often	87.5	45.8	62.5	38.6	67.9	43.5	75.0	42.4	48.7
Attention- Seeking	none	-	43.8	27.0	52.3	21.4	46.3	12.5	47.2	41.7
	some	87.5	48.6	63.5	40.9	64.3	47.2	70.8	46.4	50.3
	often	12.5	7.6	9.5	6.8	14.3	6.5	16.7	6.4	6.8

Note: Statistically significant results in italics. N=152.

personal problems that young offenders experience.

The totals in the right-hand column give some sense of the lived reality of young offenders. The percentages indicate high levels of substance abuse (23.8 percent alcohol, and 55 percent both drugs and alcohol) with a high percentage of severe alcohol and drug abuse (69.1 percent and 46.7 percent, respectively).

Table 5.6: Problems with Life Skills by Childhood Abuse

Youth Problems		Physical			Psychological			Neglect			Sexual		
		none	some	often	none	some	often	none	some	often	none	some	often
Behavioural Problems	none	7.9	-	-	11.5	-	2.0	10.4	-	2.0	6.3	-	-
	some	60.4	61.1	10.7	70.5	57.1	23.5	67.2	52.9	27.5	58.7	27.3	9.1
	often	31.7	38.9	89.3	18.0	42.9	74.5	22.4	47.1	70.6	34.9	72.7	90.9
Passivity/ Withdrawal	none	55.4	38.9	21.4	75.4	26.8	25.5	68.7	38.2	21.6	53.2	36.4	9.1
	some	39.6	38.9	53.6	24.6	56.1	54.9	28.4	47.1	58.8	37.3	45.5	72.7
	often	5.0	22.2	25.0	-	17.1	19.6	3.0	14.7	19.6	9.5	18.2	18.2
Defensive Behaviour	none	41.6	27.8	-	59.0	15.0	12.0	52.2	18.2	13.7	38.1	9.1	-
	some	40.6	55.5	50.0	36.1	57.5	44.0	37.3	48.5	51.0	45.2	36.4	54.5
	often	17.8	16.7	50.0	4.9	27.5	44.0	10.4	33.3	35.3	16.7	54.5	45.5
Verbal Aggression	none	50.5	38.9	3.6	67.2	32.5	10.0	62.7	21.2	19.6	45.2	18.1	9.1
	some	38.6	50.0	53.6	26.2	52.5	58.0	28.4	60.2	52.9	41.3	54.5	54.5
	often	10.9	11.1	42.9	6.6	15.0	32.0	9.0	18.2	27.5	13.5	27.3	36.4
Physical Aggression (others)	none	44.6	22.2	10.7	55.7	31.7	12.0	50.7	23.5	21.6	38.9	27.3	-
	some	35.6	55.6	42.9	32.8	43.9	44.0	37.3	47.1	37.3	38.1	45.5	63.6
	often	19.8	22.2	46.4	11.5	24.4	44.0	11.9	29.4	41.2	23.0	27.3	36.4
Physical Aggression (property)	none	39.6	11.2	10.7	45.9	29.3	12.0	46.3	20.6	15.7	32.5	27.3	9.1
	some	51.5	77.8	64.3	45.9	61.0	68.0	46.3	64.7	66.7	59.5	36.4	72.7
	often	8.9	11.1	25.0	8.2	9.8	20.0	7.5	14.7	17.6	7.9	36.4	18.2
Anger	none	40.6	33.3	3.6	57.4	22.5	10.0	49.3	24.2	15.7	38.9	-	-
	some	24.8	22.2	7.1	24.6	27.5	10.0	25.4	6.1	23.5	20.6	30.0	18.2
	often	34.7	44.4	89.3	18.0	50.0	80.0	25.4	69.7	60.8	40.5	70.0	81.8
Attention-Seeking	none	52.5	16.7	14.3	60.7	37.5	18.0	56.7	30.3	25.5	47.6	9.1	9.1
	some	45.5	55.6	71.4	36.1	55.0	68.0	38.3	63.6	60.8	46.8	72.2	90.0
	often	2.0	27.8	14.3	3.3	7.5	14.0	4.5	6.1	13.7	5.6	18.2	-

Note: For total percentages, see Table 5.5. Statistically significant results in italics.

Furthermore, more than 40 percent of young offenders live on the streets at least some of the time and almost 85 percent have no or low personal finances. Of all the young offenders in this sample, 11.2 percent have engaged in prostitution for financial survival and 19.1 percent have been assaulted outside of the home. The physical and emotional health of these youth seems to be relatively jeopardized. While 12 percent indicate poor levels of physical health, the levels of emotional health are distressingly low. For example, almost 24 percent of these youth have had suicidal tendencies and 9.9 percent have engaged in self-abusive behaviour, either slashing or cutting. This phenomenon of self-mutilation, or "slashing," is relatively common in long-term custodial facilities, and explanations range from theories about disempowered individuals maintaining control over at least their physical being to explanations derived from the effect of trauma on behaviour. The second argument has received support from corrections officials who see slashing in prisons as a desperate and somewhat rational attempt to relieve extreme psychic distress (Schissel 1995b; Kershaw and Lasovich 1991). In short, physical pain is used to mask the psychic pain of isolation and social deprivation. The same reasoning could easily be applied to street youth, who live mostly under conditions of oppression and social and familial isolation.

When we observe the factors that contribute to personal problems, it is interesting that parental psychiatric problems have inconsistently significant influences, mainly influencing prostitution, self-abuse and suicidal tendencies; high levels of prostitution, self-abuse and suicidal tendencies are associated with high levels of parental psychiatric problems. Furthermore, parental alcohol abuse influences all the personal problems of youth with the exception of prostitution. Again, as expected, high levels of parental alcohol abuse contribute to high levels of personal problems. Notably, 19 percent of youth with alcoholic parents have slashed or cut themselves, compared to 3.4 percent whose parents were not alcoholics. Similarly, for those with alcoholic parents, 42.9 percent have experienced suicidal tendencies (28.6 percent sometimes suicidal and 14.3 percent often suicidal), compared to 10.2 percent whose parents were not alcoholics. It is interesting, as well, that parental drinking problems have damaging effects on youths' physical health and on whether they are assaulted outside of the home.

The patterns for parental drug abuse are similar, except that parental drug abuse does not appear to influence physical health, self-abuse or suicidal tendencies to any significant degree. However, it does influence prostitution to a considerable degree. For those youths whose parents are drug abusers, 21.4 percent have engaged in prostitution, against 7.3 percent of youth whose parents are not drug abusers. Quite expectedly, both high levels of drug and alcohol abuse among parents contribute to high levels of substance abuse among their offspring. Last, the influences of marital discord are mixed and somewhat unconvincing. Discord appears to affect youth substance abuse primarily, with higher levels of discord contributing to higher and more severe levels of abuse. Table 5.8 extends this analysis by assessing the influences of childhood abuse on personal problems.

Overall, the influences of all types of abuse seem pervasive and consistent. All four types contribute to youth substance abuse and to high levels of severity for both drug and alcohol abuse. Similarly, high levels of parental abuse in all four categories lead to a greater likelihood of youths living on the streets and a greater likelihood that their personal finances will be inadequate. However, only

Table 5.7: Personal Problems by Parental Problems

Youth Problems		Psychiatric		Alcohol		Drugs		Marital Discord		Total
		Parental Problems								
		yes	no	yes	no	yes	no	yes	no	
Substance	none	14.3	21.5	*11.1*	*28.4*	*3.6*	*25.2*	*4.2*	*25.8*	21.2
Abuse	alcohol	14.3	24.3	*14.3*	*30.7*	*14.3*	*26.8*	*20.8*	*25.0*	23.8
	alc. + drugs	71.4	54.2	*74.6*	*40.9*	*82.1*	*48.0*	*75.0*	*49.2*	55.0
Severity of	low	25.0	31.3	*15.6*	*42.0*	*7.1*	*36.3*	*8.3*	*36.0*	30.9
Alc. Abuse	high	75.0	68.8	*84.4*	*58.0*	*92.9*	*63.7*	*91.7*	*64.0*	69.1
Severity of	low	50.0	53.5	*33.3*	*67.0*	28.6	59.3	29.2	59.2	53.3
Drug Abuse	high	50.0	46.5	*66.7*	*33.0*	71.4	40.7	70.8	40.8	46.7
Living on	none	37.6	61.6	*46.0*	*70.5*	35.7	65.9	45.8	61.6	59.9
the Streets	some	25.0	23.6	*30.2*	*19.3*	35.7	20.3	25.0	23.2	23.7
	often	37.5	15.3	*23.8*	*10.2*	28.6	13.8	29.2	15.2	16.4
Finances	no	12.5	17.3	*16.1*	*16.7*	14.3	38.7	8.0	20.2	18.0
	low	87.5	66.2	*77.4*	*60.7*	82.1	63.6	76.0	63.9	66.7
	adequate	-	16.5	*6.5*	*22.6*	3.6	18.6	16.0	16.0	15.3
Pros-	no	*62.6*	*91.7*	87.3	93.2	78.6	*92.7*	79.2	*91.9*	88.8
titution	yes	*37.5*	*8.3*	12.7	6.8	*21.4*	*7.3*	*20.8*	*8.1*	11.2
Assaulted	no	75.0	81.3	*73.0*	*86.4*	64.3	85.4	66.7	*84.8*	80.9
Out of	yes	25.0	18.8	*27.0*	*13.6*	35.7	14.6	33.3	*15.2*	19.1
Home										
Physical	poor	12.5	11.1	*12.7*	*10.2*	10.7	11.4	8.3	11.2	11.8
Health	moderate	62.5	45.8	*65.1*	*34.1*	64.3	42.3	45.8	47.2	46.7
	very good	25.9	43.1	*22.2*	*55.7*	25.0	46.3	45.8	41.6	41.4
Self-	no	*62.5*	*91.7*	*81.0*	*96.9*	82.1	91.9	79.2	92.0	90.1
Abuse	yes	*37.5*	*8.3*	*19.0*	*3.4*	17.9	8.1	20.8	8.0	9.9
(Slashing)										
Suicidal	none	*25.0*	*79.2*	*57.1*	*89.8*	60.7	79.7	66.7	79.2	76.2
Tendencies	some	*75.0*	*12.5*	*28.6*	*6.8*	28.6	13.0	25.0	13.6	15.9
	often	-	*8.3*	*14.3*	*3.4*	10.7	7.3	8.3	7.2	7.9

Note: Statistically significant results in italics. N=152.

sexual abuse has an effect on whether youths engage in prostitution. This somewhat expected result is supported by a rather large body of literature that argues that childhood sexual activity is a predisposing condition to sexual exploitation in adulthood (cf. Shaver 1993; Earls and David 1990; Lowman 1989, 1991).

Interestingly, the non-physical forms of abuse (psychological and neglect) are associated with the physical health of youth and, along with sexual abuse, contribute to higher levels of victimization from assault outside the home. The emotional health of these adolescents is related to all forms of childhood abuse: higher levels of abuse lead to higher levels of self-abuse and suicidal tendencies. The differences in percentages for suicidal tendencies are marked evidence of the relationship between abuse and emotional health. For example, 3.2 percent of the youth who have never been sexually assaulted have suicidal tendencies, compared to 36.4 percent of those who have been. The other forms of abuse display the same patterns. Concerning self-abuse, 6.3 percent of those who have never been sexually assaulted at home have slashed or cut themselves. For those youth who have been sexually assaulted, 45.5 percent have hurt themselves. These percentages are startling and convincing evidence that childhood victimization contributes significantly to the emotional damage of children. And it is understandable that emotional trauma can either predispose kids to legal involvement or possibly result from legal processing and punishment.

Legal Problems and Family Life

The last two tables in this chapter illustrate what was just mentioned about predisposing kids to legal experiences and sanctions. Table 5.9 shows the associations between parental problems and legal outcomes for the youth in this study.

The legal problems listed are intended to indicate the severity of legal sanction and disobedience experienced by the youths and how their non-legal behaviour may result from being victims of damaging childhood experiences. "Non-compliance with authority" and "running to escape custody" are common official youth crimes, especially since the implementation of the Young Offenders Act, and are more indicative of the inability of the courts to deal with youth offenders than with the criminal intentions of youths. The variable "improvement in attitude and behaviour" is an assessment by social services and court officials as to the rehabilitative progress of the particular youth and gives some sense of how previous life trauma affects the healing process. "Income by theft" is intended to show whether this specific illegal act is the result of criminal predisposition (we hear often in political and news rhetoric that criminal families create criminal youths) or whether youth theft is an act of survival.

If we look at the "income by theft," it is clear that, with the exception of "marital discord," none of the parental problems has a significant effect on theft. As we will see in Table 5.10, the same holds true for the affects of childhood

Table 5.8. Personal Problems by Childhood

ABUSE

Youth Problems		Physical			Psychological			Neglect			Sexual		
		none	some	often	none	some	often	none	some	often	none	some	often
Substance	none	27.7	5.6	18.5	36.1	7.5	18.4	35.8	12.1	12.0	26.2	9.1	-
Abuse	alcohol	*27.7*	*33.3*	*3.7*	*31.3*	*35.9*	*6.1*	*29.9*	*21.2*	*18.0*	*27.0*	*18.2*	-
	alc+drug	*44.6*	*61.6*	*77.8*	*32.8*	*57.5*	*75.7*	*34.3*	*66.7*	*70.0*	*46.8*	*72.7*	*100*
Severity of	low	*37.6*	*16.7*	*28.6*	*47.5*	*17.5*	*26.0*	*49.3*	*21.2*	*17.6*	*36.5*	*9.1*	*18.2*
Alc. Abuse	high	*62.4*	*83.3*	*71.4*	*52.5*	*82.5*	*74.0*	*50.7*	*78.8*	*82.4*	*63.5*	*90.9*	*81.8*
Severity of	low	*61.4*	*44.4*	*42.9*	*73.8*	*52.5*	*34.0*	*71.6*	*39.4*	*43.1*	*61.1*	*36.4*	*18.2*
Drug Abuse	high	*38.6*	*55.6*	*57.1*	*26.2*	*47.5*	*66.0*	*28.4*	*60.6*	*56.9*	*38.9*	*63.6*	*81.1*
Living on	none	*64.4*	*77.8*	*32.1*	*77.0*	*53.7*	*40.0*	*76.1*	*45.7*	*43.1*	*65.9*	*30.0*	*27.3*
the Streets	some	*19.8*	*16.7*	*35.7*	*11.5*	*36.6*	*28.0*	*17.9*	*34.3*	*25.5*	*20.6*	*50.0*	*27.3*
	often	*15.8*	*5.6*	*32.1*	*11.5*	*9.8*	*32.0*	*6.0*	*20.0*	*31.4*	*13.5*	*20.0*	*45.5*
Finances	no	*24.7*	-	*11.1*	*18.6*	*24.4*	*12.2*	*15.4*	*21.9*	*19.6*	*19.8*	*18.2*	-
	low	*52.6*	*100*	*85.2*	*52.5*	*65.9*	*83.7*	*56.9*	*62.5*	*80.4*	*61.2*	*81.8*	*100*
	adequate	*22.7*	-	-	*28.8*	*9.8*	*4.1*	*27.7*	*15.6*	-	*19.0*	-	-
Pros-	no	93.0	94.4	75.0	96.7	90.2	80.0	98.5	85.7	78.4	*96.0*	*70.0*	*36.4*
titution	yes	7.0	5.6	25.0	3.3	9.8	20.0	1.5	14.3	21.6	*4.0*	*30.0*	*63.6*
Assaulted	no	87.1	72.7	71.4	*93.4*	*80.0*	*68.0*	*92.5*	*75.8*	*70.6*	*84.1*	*50.0*	*63.6*
Out of	yes	12.9	27.8	28.6	*6.6*	*20.0*	*32.0*	*7.5*	*24.2*	*29.4*	*15.9*	*50.0*	*36.4*
Home													
Physical	poor	9.9	16.7	14.3	*6.6*	*24.4*	*8.0*	*13.4*	*6.1*	*11.8*	10.3	27.3	9.1
Health	moderate	42.6	55.6	53.6	*41.0*	*39.0*	*60.0*	*34.3*	*54.5*	*58.8*	45.2	54.5	63.6
	very good	47.5	27.8	32.1	*52.5*	*36.6*	*32.0*	*52.2*	*39.4*	*29.4*	44.4	18.2	27.3
Self-	no	*95.0*	*83.3*	*75.0*	*98.4*	*92.7*	*78.0*	*97.0*	*94.1*	*78.4*	*93.7*	*100*	*54.5*
Abuse	yes	*5.0*	*16.7*	*25.0*	*1.6*	*7.3*	*22.0*	*3.0*	*5.9*	*21.6*	*6.3*	-	*45.5*
(Slashing)													
Suicidal	none	*85.1*	*77.8*	*46.4*	*91.8*	*75.0*	*60.0*	*85.1*	*81.8*	*62.7*	*84.9*	*60.0*	*9.1*
Tendencies	some	*8.9*	*22.2*	*35.7*	*8.2*	*15.0*	*26.0*	*10.4*	*9.1*	*27.5*	*11.9*	*30.0*	*54.5*
	often	*5.9*	-	*17.9*	-	*10.0*	*14.0*	*4.5*	*9.1*	*9.8*	*3.2*	*10.0*	*36.4*

Note: For total percentages, see Table 5.7. Statistically significant results in italics. N=152.

abuse on theft. One might reasonably speculate that the act of theft has little relation to family and childhood trauma and much more to do with economic survival and possibly youth rebellion. Given the high percentage of youths in this study who have committed acts of theft (73.4 percent for "some" theft and 8.4 percent for "often") it is likely that many of these acts are not pathologically determined but the result of privation and disadvantage (and consequently individual need) or peer culture behaviour.

The other legal variables in this study, however, are more closely associated with parental problems. For example, the amount of time a youth spends in custody results—most likely indirectly—from all four types of parental problems. Most noticeably, psychiatric problems have a strong effect on time in custody (83.3 percent for those with parental psychiatric problems, compared to 26.2 percent for those with no parental psychiatric problems, among those in custody for "six months or more"); so does parental alcohol abuse (52 percent versus 14.3 percent). The effects of psychiatric problems are evident, as well, for non-compliance to authority and running to escape custody. It is significant that these relatively innocuous acts of defiance or desperation are associated with family problems.

Table 5.10 assesses further the traumatic effects of damaging family experiences by correlating childhood abuse with legal outcomes. The results for this table are unambiguous and illustrative of the harmful legal effects of childhood victimization. All forms of abuse result in higher levels of incarceration, defiance of authority and running to escape custody. And, with the exception of sexual abuse, all forms of abuse block the rehabilitation process. Last, as we saw in Table 5.9, childhood family experiences have little or no effect on theft. Once again, we might suggest that theft is not an act of criminal disposition or intent but more likely an act of survival or rebellion.

Conclusion

The conclusion I am forced to reach from these statistical analyses stands in bold contradiction to Canada's moral panic about youth crime. Simply put, the logic and rhetoric of politics and news is so flawed and poorly struck that malicious intentions cannot be dismissed. This look at the reality of youth crime shows that there is no substance to the contention that youths are progressively becoming more criminal and more dangerous. If there are gun-toting mall prowlers, they are a minuscule minority.

First, it is important to reiterate that youth crime rates are largely a function of the structure and nature of legal practice and not of increases or decreases in actual crimes committed. Moreover, the street youth survey shows that most street kids (and especially Aboriginal youth) are in trouble for violations of the formal bureaucratic rules of the Young Offenders Act, and are not the gun-toting kids pictured in *Maclean's* and *Alberta Report*. To those who argue that the Young Offenders Act is allowing youths to "get away with murder," I would say

Table 5.9. Legal Problems by Parental Problems

Youth Problems		Psychiatric yes	Psychiatric no	Alcohol yes	Alcohol no	Drugs yes	Drugs no	Marital Discord yes	Marital Discord no	Total
Time in	none	-	*50.8*	*28.0*	*61.0*	*21.7*	*55.2*	*25.0*	*54.1*	48.5
Custody	to 6 mos	*16.7*	*23.0*	*20.0*	*24.7*	*30.4*	*20.0*	*25.0*	*22.0*	22.7
	+ 6 mos	*83.3*	*26.2*	*52.0*	*14.3*	*47.8*	*24.8*	*50.0*	*23.9*	28.8
Income by	none	12.5	18.1	13.8	19.5	17.2	17.9	*8.0*	*21.0*	18.2
Theft	some	87.5	72.9	73.8	74.7	72.4	74.0	*72.0*	*73.4*	73.4
	often	-	9.0	12.3	5.7	10.3	8.1	*20.0*	*5.6*	8.4
Non-	none	-	*13.8*	*3.0*	*20.5*	3.4	15.2	8.0	15.2	13.0
compliance	some	*12.5*	*26.9*	*25.8*	*28.4*	20.7	28.0	16.0	26.4	27.3
Authority	often	*87.5*	*59.3*	*71.2*	*51.1*	75.9	56.8	76.0	58.4	59.7
Runs to	none	12.5	*38.2*	*20.3*	*50.0*	*21.4*	*40.8*	20.8	40.0	37.0
Escape	some	-	*34.0*	*31.3*	*33.0*	*25.0*	*33.6*	37.5	31.2	32.5
Custody	often	*87.5*	*27.8*	*48.4*	*17.0*	*53.6*	*25.6*	41.7	28.8	30.5
Improve-	none	75.0	44.4	*57.8*	*36.4*	53.6	44.0	50.0	46.4	46.1
ment	some	25.0	43.8	*31.3*	*51.5*	39.3	43.2	50.0	40.8	42.9
Attitude	often	-	11.8	*10.9*	*12.5*	7.1	12.8	-	12.8	11.0
Behaviour										

Note: Statistically significant results in italics. N=154.

that nothing could be farther from the truth. The trends in informal and formal rates of arrests, charges and convictions suggest that the legal system is, in fact, becoming more punitive. Second, the increases documented in the press and political speeches are evident for both youth and adult crime statistics. Last, with regard to crime rate trends, there is little evidence that female youth are becoming more criminal and more like male youth in their orientations to criminal behaviour.

The data on the culture of street youth provide considerable clarity about the connections between socio-economic marginalization, stereotyping and harsh and inadequate justice. It is clear that street youth face high arrest rates and are often legally disadvantaged. Their legal rights are often abrogated with respect to presence of counsel, presence of guardians and awareness of their legal rights. Although street youth do receive sentences like diversion and mediation, which are in accordance with the provisions of the YOA, Aboriginal youth are less likely than non-Aboriginal youth to receive lenient sentences and are more likely to be sentenced to closed custody. Finally, when we observe socio-

Table 5.10. Legal Problems by Childhood Abuse

		Abuse											
Youth Problems		**Physical**			**Psychological**			**Neglect**			**Sexual**		
		none	some	often	none	some	often	none	some	often	none	some	often
Time in	none	*64.0*	*37.5*	*12.5*	*79.6*	*48.6*	*14.6*	*75.4*	*35.7*	*27.3*	*57.1*	*27.3*	*10.0*
Custody	6 mos	*22.1*	*18.8*	*20.8*	*13.0*	*25.7*	*26.8*	*14.0*	*28.6*	*25.0*	*21.0*	*36.4*	*30.0*
	+6 mos	*14.0*	*43.8*	*66.7*	*7.4*	*25.7*	*58.5*	*10.5*	*35.7*	*47.7*	*21.9*	*36.4*	*60.0*
Income by	none	22.0	5.6	17.9	25.0	16.7	11.5	19.7	17.1	17.3	18.4	20.0	27.3
Theft	some	72.0	77.8	71.4	71.7	71.4	76.9	75.8	77.1	67.3	74.4	70.0	72.7
	often	6.0	16.7	10.7	3.3	11.9	11.5	4.5	5.7	15.4	7.2	10.0	-
Non-	none	*19.8*	-	*3.6*	*26.2*	*4.8*	*5.8*	*25.4*	*8.6*	*1.9*	*16.7*	-	-
compliance	some	*27.7*	*44.4*	*3.6*	*32.8*	*33.3*	*15.4*	*31.3*	*25.7*	*21.2*	*27.0*	*27.3*	*18.2*
Authority	often	*52.5*	*55.6*	*92.9*	*41.0*	*61.9*	*78.8*	*43.4*	*65.7*	*76.9*	*56.3*	*72.7*	*81.8*
Runs to	none	*48.5*	*27.8*	*7.1*	*60.7*	*28.6*	*18.0*	*61.2*	*22.9*	*15.7*	*42.9*	*27.3*	*9.1*
Escape	some	*31.7*	*44.4*	*21.4*	*27.9*	*45.2*	*26.0*	*31.3*	*42.9*	*27.5*	*32.5*	*27.3*	*18.2*
	often	*19.8*	*27.8*	*71.4*	*11.5*	*26.2*	*56.0*	*7.5*	*34.3*	*56.9*	*24.6*	*45.5*	*72.7*
Improve-	none	*41.6*	*33.3*	*67.9*	*39.3*	*38.1*	*58.0*	*35.8*	*44.1*	*58.8*	44.4	36.4	72.7
ment	some	*42.6*	*61.6*	*32.1*	*41.0*	*50.0*	*42.0*	*44.8*	*50.0*	*37.3*	42.9	54.5	27.3
Attitude	often	*15.8*	*5.6*	-	*19.7*	*11.9*	-	*19.4*	*5.9*	*3.9*	12.7	9.1	-
Behaviour													

Note: For total percentages, see Table 5.9. Statistically signifcant results in italics. N=154.

economic and personal profiles of street youth, it is clear that they are often isolated from family, they are often treated poorly by the police and their socio-economic situations are meagre. Interestingly, these youth appear to find decent and fair treatment in custodial institutions. Other realities for street youth include prostitution as a survival mechanism, high levels of alcohol and drug abuse—very much associated to their being arrested—and relationships with others who are arrested. Contrary to public sentiment, street youths are not typically from broken families or single-parent families; the majority are from two-parent-nuclear or extended families.

The social/personal profile of street youth is also important because it identifies the connections of gender, race and class with legal and social disadvantage. In general, the greatest disadvantages accrue to Aboriginal youths, to female youths in some respects and male youths in others, and to the poorest and wealthiest youths on the street.

The final investigation of the sample of youths who have been arrested clarifies the connection of social and personal victimization with legal difficulties. The results are unambiguous and persuasive. Parental problems, both volitional and non-volitional, lead to high levels of personality problems in youth, especially problems of violence and aggression. Similarly, various forms of child abuse, almost without exception, produce personality problems, and the most extreme results appear for physical and sexual abuse.

As with personality problems, parental problems and childhood abuse produce inordinately high levels of substance abuse, self-injurious behaviour, social isolation, poor physical and mental health, low incomes and involvement in prostitution. These consistent results suggest irrefutably that statutory youth are inordinately victimized and that their victimization leads to dangerous and detrimental behaviour and situations.

Our analysis of legalized youth also illustrates how victimization leads to legal disadvantage and victimization. Both high levels of parental problems and childhood abuse lead to greater time in custody, greater likelihood of defying the courts and lesser chance of rehabilitation. Interestingly, family problems seem not to determine involvement in theft, again suggesting that theft is mostly a survival mechanism.

The empirical results found in this chapter argue clearly for an enlightened approach to youth crime that defies the contention that youth are progressively evil, that their deviant behaviour is inexplicable and unpredictable, and that they present a danger to society. The results suggest a need for greater sensitivity to the vulnerable and perilous situations many disadvantaged youth find themselves in. To argue that there is a need to further punish youth offenders, many of whom have been punished all their lives, is ill-informed and unfounded on empirical findings.

Chapter 6

Understanding Child-Hating

Two theoretical issues inform this book. The first falls under the broad rubric of social constructionism and assumes that public images of acceptable behaviour and appropriate penalties for violations of social norms are highly variable, as is the definition of "normal" behaviour. As a result, what constitutes "deviant" behaviour changes over time and across social groups and societies. The social-constructionist approach is informed largely by historical studies that have tracked changing modes of social control. And it is almost axiomatic that moral panics occur in troubled times. As we observe the public and political venom directed towards children and youths, and as we contextualize youth misconduct in the structure, culture and family of contemporary society, we are left with the gnawing question of "What is going on?" at this particular time. My focus, then, is on how power operates in defining and sanctioning virtuous and evil behaviours among youth. The second theoretical concern attempts to understand the origins and intent of such power. The presumption is that collective fear becomes highly politicized as it is manipulated either inadvertently or deliberately for political and economic ends.

In Chapter 1, I presented a series of theoretical positions for understanding Canada's current moral panic about youth and, in light of the two theoretical orientations above, I return to them to make sense of the paradox between child victimization and child blaming. On one level, these explanations seem inadequate because they do not answer why many youths who suffer economic, social and personal privation go on to become law-abiding and productive citizens. And, of course, much of the rhetoric of law and order is based on the presumption that everybody at one time or another has suffered victimization, but only the truly bad engage in criminal behaviour. What these sociological positions address, however, is how a stratified society, by causing people to live on the margins, not only creates criminal behaviour but constructs certain types of behaviour and persons as unacceptable, not on the basis of inherent morality, but on the basis of social signifiers.

The Sociology of Knowledge and the Deconstruction of Crime Myths

It is important to focus on fear and the knowledge than underpins that fear. As social analysts, we are forced to confront the task of deconstructing public opinion, which we assume to be based on selected and biased knowledge. Further, we need to uncover the sources of information and to assess the claims to legitimacy—or, in journalistic parlance, to objectivity—that inform and direct public opinion. Cohen (1980:28) has made us aware that public opinion fluctuates and that it may cause social reform:

> Societies appear to be subject, every now and then, to periods of moral panic. A condition, episode, person or group of persons emerges to become defined as a threat to societal values and interests: its nature is presented in a stylized and stereo-typical fashion by the mass media: the moral barricades are manned by editors, bishops, politicians and other right-thinking people; socially accredited experts pronounce their diagnoses and solutions. . . . Sometimes the panic is passed over and is forgotten, except in folklore and collective memory; at other times it has more serious and long lasting repercussions and might produce such changes as those in legal and social policy or even in the way society conceives itself.

The massive and biased coverage of Canada's youth criminals and pre-criminals by the press and politicians bears witness to the stability, persistence and power of the war against youth crime.

Social constructionism, as part of the domain of post-modernism, is based on the methodological position that "[d]econstruction tears a text (all phenomena, all events, are texts) apart, [and] reveals its contradictions and assumptions" (Rosenau 1992). The questions we need to ask are: What are the hidden messages that "objective journalism" conveys? Who are the originators of such ideological communiqués and how do they make claims to legitimacy? Who are the expressed and insinuated targets of the social/political attack?

Our discussions in Chapters 3 and 4 show that the recurring focus in media and political accounts of youth crime is on people who live on the margins. The manifest messages are that society is too lenient with children and that the only way to restore public safety and appropriate conduct is to become "tough" about law and order. The associated belief is that kids are inherently evil and that discipline and punishment are essential to the creation of normal, law-abiding children. The latent messages are much more damning: youths who break laws are said to belong to certain racial and ethnic categories, to have been born and raised in the lower socio-economic strata of society, to come from feminized families, and to lack morality because of their socio-economic positions in society. Simply put, the messages indict poverty and endorse wealth, and blame the poor for being poor, condemn mothers almost exclusively for poor parenting and censure cultural difference as criminogenic.

The work of Foucault (1980) is particularly instructive in understanding the nature of discourse surrounding young offenders. For Foucault, discourses are

historically variable ways of specifying knowledge and truth—what it is possible to speak of at a given moment. They function (especially scientific discourses) as sets of rules, and the operation of these rules and concepts in programmes which specify what is or is not the case—what constitutes insanity, for example. Discourses are, therefore, powerful. Those who are labelled insane, or hysterical women or frigid wives, are in the grip of power. This power may be exercised by officials through institutions, or through many other practices, but power is constituted in discourses and it is in discourses, such as those in clinical medicine, that power lies. Discourses produce truths and "we cannot exercise power except through the production of truth." (Foucault, cited in Ramazanoglu 1993:10)

Foucault argues that historical periods are marked by particular discourses that constrain the types of knowledge produced. Within historical periods knowledge is constructed and deployed on the basis of what types of people have access to systems of knowledge, and it is this access to "legitimate knowledge" that gives people their power.

The basic tenets of the Foucauldian power/knowledge perspective are evident in the discourse about youth offenders described in Chapters 3 and 4. The ways of speaking about young offenders are restricted largely to individual or family-based accounts of the origins of crime. Rarely are the explanations based on structural inequalities or the injustices people suffer while living on the margins of society. As Foucault (1980) has suggested, the discourses of historical periods are constrictive; they are rules under which "talk" can be carried out. And it appears that the modern discourse about youth crime and punishment is restricted to accounts based on individual blame. This contemporary medical/psychological discourse of goodness and badness sets youth crime in a context of orthodox criminology: individuals gone wrong, either inherently or culturally. The underlying ideological position is that society is structured correctly and that individuals who offend are individually or socially pathological and identifiable.

The discourse of individual or cultural blame receives its legitimacy primarily through the knowledge of experts. The language and accounts of youth criminality are often the products of testimonials by "scientists." Discourse operates as a powerful and, I would argue, oppressive mechanism because it comes from the mouths of "legitimated speakers" who are almost without exception drawn from the privileged sectors of society. As our analysis of news accounts has shown, news articles are often infused with the voices of "professionals" who corroborate their claims. This strategy not only endorses the validity of the accounts, but it gives the media legitimacy by association. Furthermore, the "expert wisdom" of legitimated speakers is often accompanied by the folk wisdom of "ordinary people," and it is this technique of attaching common knowledge to expert knowledge that produces an atmosphere of credibility.

In his treatises on power and knowledge, Foucault (1980) was generally unconcerned with the origins of discourses and what interests they served. Typical of post-modern orientations, his approach to the study of the social construction of truth focuses on how power and knowledge operate—not on what discourses mean but on what makes them possible. As a consequence, this approach leaves us with the crucial problem of who controls the images of youth, who benefits from biased and incriminating portraits of offenders and why certain categories of people are the targets of journalistic and political abuse. To answer these questions we need to turn to critical-feminist- and political-economy-based theories of knowledge as they relate to criminality and use them to achieve some insights into the rhetoric of child-hating.

Feminist Theory and the Construction of Gendered Images

Law-and-order campaigns, as we have seen in previous chapters, are in part veiled attacks on women and feminism. Media presentations maintain that women are more susceptible to victimization and poverty than men, but that they also, through inadequate parenting, are producers of criminality. In essence, women are said to be the inadvertent victimizers of children. Such stereotypical and conventional explanations of criminality have focused on non-traditional families, non-traditional motherhood, single-parenthood and poverty as causal factors in youth criminality. Feminism's response to conservative, traditional explanations of crime is that patriarchal ideologies frame the nature of women's crime and the imputed female role in criminogenesis. Feminism, as a generic theoretical position, is highly complex and multidimensional, and feminist studies generally address the structure of society as disadvantageous to women; in patriarchal societies, men inhabit positions of privilege and domination over women. Furthermore, in such societies, women and men live in different experiential worlds, and the knowledge that underpins our understanding of gender issues is largely produced by men and is based on stereotypical and distorted ideas about women and men. And, importantly for this book, these stereotypical "sexist" images are reproduced in the media and in academic institutions. As Anderson suggests:

> Although these institutions are not the exclusive sources of sexist ideas, they exert a powerful influence on the way we define reality and women's role within it. . . . In fact, it can be argued that in a highly complex technological-industrial society, these systems of communication and knowledge making play an increasingly important part in the generation and transmission of ideas. . . . Moreover, as the feminist movement has shown, images of women conveyed by the media and in educational materials have been based on distortions and stereotypes that legitimate the status quo at the same time that they falsely represent the actual experience of women in the society. Thus, the ideas

we acquire regarding gender relations poorly prepare us for the realities we will face. (1988:25)

As we saw in Chapters 3 and 4, public images of typical delinquents are primarily about males. When female youth are targeted, the depictions are couched in "paradox talk": it is so unusual for girls to act aggressively or antisocially that bad genes must be at work. The "sugar and spice" understanding of femaleness is often the standard upon which young female offenders are judged and, in effect, the images of "bad girls" are presented as biological anomalies and/or sinister products of the feminist movement. A general woman-hatred appears to underlie the "sugar and spice" conception of femaleness in articles that discuss the wild, passionate and out-of-character woman who has to be constrained or held back, revealing a dual stereotype of women in Western society—nice but emotional and unpredictable.

A second way women are included and loathed in media accounts of youth crime is through speculations about the causal origins of delinquent behaviour. Specifically, references are made to "feminist women" who are trying to be like men and to the inability of single mothers to raise "normal children" within the confines of an "abnormal family" living in conditions of privation. Importantly, the "family values" jargon that has become so much a part of the conservative political creed is infused with references to the functional two-parent hetero-sexual family and the importance of male discipline and male role models. Interestingly, on the basis of empirical evidence on street youths and youths who have been in contact with the courts, single-parent families show little correlation with lawbreaking behaviour, although living a life of poverty, which often is typical for single mothers, is a predisposing condition to contact with the law. Problems resulting from structural inequality and the potential unfairness of a market-based economy are attributed to problems of mothering and, ultimately, to problems created by feminism.

A feminist approach to the social construction of public knowledge is important for locating sources of bias against women in the patriarchal structures that support media, politics, academia/education and economy. Condemnatory images of women are clearly created and deployed in a rhetoric of fear, inherent criminality and unnatural predispositions; the constructed and gendered knowledge about youth crime originates in patriarchal political and economic systems.

Left Realism and the Victim/Offender Dialectic

"Left Realism," as a Marxist-based theory of crime and justice, is concerned with the way crime becomes defined by powerful people in association with the state political system. One of the tenets of Left Realism is that traditional legal understandings of crime and guilt are made without considering the role or the welfare of the victim. But victimization is important because crime panics largely play to people's innate fear of crime and every citizen's potential victimization. However, the Left Realist maxim of "taking crime seriously" also suggests that, before society can address socio-economic issues that underpin disparities in criminal behaviour and judicial outcomes, it must understand and deal with the immediate needs of those most at risk to criminal victimization. This focus on victimization is based on the assumptions that much criminal behaviour is largely intraclass and intrarace; people are mostly victimized by and fearful of associates or people in the same social environment. This empirical focus on victimization is insightful, given that moral panics play on a fear of "others," when the reality is that victimization is usually intragroup (c.f. Lowman and MacLean [1992] for Left Realism and crime control, and MacLean and Milovanovic [1991] for post-modern orientations in Left Realism).

The concept of the victim is important in this book for three reasons. First, the reality that when youths break the law, they generally victimize others like themselves, stands in stark contrast to the public perception that youths are becoming pervasively dangerous. This phenomenon is especially true for race; gang members, for example, generally offend against each other (although "gang" has become a code word for "race" and a legitimate way of expressing racism without the racial epithets). Second, public accounts of youth crime often focus on the victim in attempts to invoke sympathy, empathy and fear in the reader; this victim-based account is most often done when the victim is not typical. Third, many youths who get into trouble with the law have been previously victimized and their victimization predisposes them not only to legal scrutiny but also to excessive socio-economic disadvantage.

The realist position alerts us to how the concept of victimization can be misused. Research shows that a life on the margins of society exposes youths to danger. They are in danger from street exploitation, from family and peer violence, from legal exploitation and, in many cases, from themselves. This complex net of victimization is rarely dealt with in public accounts of youth crime. The proposition of "victim first, offender second" is ignored, especially at the applied social-policy level. The Young Offenders Act is based on understanding the exploitative and marginalized background of many offenders, but the reality is that the law is often not applied with this in mind, and certainly the new wave of conservative law-and-order politics vehemently denies the usefulness of thinking in such terms.

Ironically, media and political accounts of youth crime turn victimization on its head by redefining and recontextualizing the victimized as the victimizer. Even more enlightened responses to crime, such as mediation and healing, rarely recognize the history of abuse that many offenders experience. These contemporary, legal alternatives emphasize offender responsibility and citizenship, and tend to ignore youths as victims first and offenders second. In fact, youth offenders may be accurately described as *survivors* who are punished by law for offenses viewed out of context. Unfortunately, the public and state responses to this statement are that it offers little hope for rehabilitation whereas accepting responsibility and showing contrition do.

Consistent with the tenets of Left Realist criminology, I would offer that state policy can have an influence in reducing discrimination and injustice for young offenders, despite the patriarchal and stratified nature of society. Several things, however, must be assured. First, the principle of individual responsibility is important, but it must be offered in a context in which the community and the society reflect about, and work to resolve, the injustices inherent in a society stratified according to socio-economic class. For example, when youths are judged officially by the courts and unofficially by public opinion, the unjust nature of the social structure is largely ignored. That youths need to survive somehow is the appropriate context in which to discuss youth crime. I ask you to recall the example of the eleven-year-old boy in Chicago who was killed in a gangland slaying. The crux of the article was that he was the victim of circumstance and that, despite his social circumstances, he could have survived if he simply had not chosen to become involved in gang activity. This sentiment is echoed in many other media accounts of crime: if only the offender would have avoided certain criminogenic circumstances. What these accounts miss, however, is that, like the youth in Chicago and the typical street youth, adolescents need affiliations, security and unqualified support. If these needs are not met in one context, they must seek them elsewhere. Such youths are not evil and dangerous, they are simply trying to survive in a less than perfect world. Social policy needs to constantly reflect on and address the imperfections and dangers of a capitalistic society. This is where Left Realism recaptures its Marxist roots and how it incorporates victimization as a fundamental consideration in just and equitable social policy.

Second, Left Realism offers that reforms to the existing social and economic systems can be more than token if changes come about through the energies and political will of people who are relatively marginalized. This "working class-based" social policy strategy has important implications for youth law reform. Legal and social welfare approaches to youth in general, and young offenders specifically, must start with the needs of the immediate community. Policy struck outside the community will necessarily have a repressive dimension because of the authoritarian nature of politics and the connections between political power and wealth. Furthermore, communities are often culturally distinct entities that have different needs, values and customs than the dominant political-economic system. What this requires is a return to community- and culture-based methods of legal resolution and we see the seminal stages of this movement in Aboriginal healing circles and community alternatives to youth incarceration.

Ideology, Power and Images of Youth

The one theoretical orientation that addresses the issue of the domination of powerful people over less powerful people as a primary focus can be subsumed under the broad category of "Marxist or Conflict Criminology." Within the various incarnations of Marxist-based theories, including the instrumentalist and structuralist, the primary assumption is that certain groups of people gain advantage over others and dominate by virtue of their position of privilege and ownership in the system of production. In this book, then, we are concerned not only with the nature of the images of youth but also with understanding the creators of those images and who is advantaged and disadvantaged by the social construction of knowledge. Obviously, the media are partly responsible for the creation and reproduction of the stratified socio-economic order by their creation of images of good and evil that are attached accordingly to preferred and non-preferred groups of people.

The "Instrumental Marxist" argument (Quinney 1974; Goff and Reasons 1978) suggests that powerful people directly influence government policy and manipulate this policy to their advantage. Government, then, is government for the wealthy and powerful, and this understanding of power and politics is difficult to envision in societies based on a democratic process. The "Structural Marxist" approach (Poulantzas 1972; Balbus 1973) argues that the state is relatively autonomous from power brokers, but that the role of the state is to create and maintain the conditions under which capital accumulation works most efficiently. In so doing, the state must create conditions under which the system of capital accumulation is held legitimate by the populace, otherwise the democratic process would likely dictate the end of a system based on domination and subordination. This is where the question of the ideological role of the media needs to be raised:

> The media, then, do not simply "create" the news; nor do they simply transmit the ideology of the "ruling class" in a conspiratorial fashion. Indeed, we have suggested, in a critical sense, the media are frequently not the "primary definers" of news events at all; but their structured relationship to power has the effect of making them play a crucial but secondary role in reproducing the definitions of those who have privileged access, as of right, to the media as "accredited sources." (Hall et al. 1978:59)

Hall and his colleagues (1978) took this structural Marxist position and applied it to the moral panics surrounding "mugging" in England in the 1960s and 1970s. They illustrated how the raw materials of crime facts get filtered to the media and are produced as "factual" stories that ultimately serve to reproduce the ideologies of powerful people.

I have sought to illustrate how stereotypical images of race, class and gender are created and employed to produce versions of goodness and badness attributable to class position. The obvious question is why do news definers and makers conform to the dominant ideology of a modern-day "ruling class," especially when the professed mandate of the media is objectivity and journalistic integrity?

Ownership

As we observe the ownership patterns of the Canadian news media, it is increasingly obvious that newspapers and news magazines are monopolized by a few major corporate interests. For example, I noted in a previous chapter that at the time of writing this book, Hollinger Corporation, owned by the Conrad Black empire, purchased the *Saskatoon Star Phoenix,* the *Regina Leader Poster* and the *Yorkton This Week and Enterprise* to become the sole owner of all daily newspapers in the province of Saskatchewan. Further, at the time, Hollinger owned approximately 60 percent of all the daily newspapers in Canada. The takeover in Saskatchewan, similar to what has occurred in other areas of Canada, resulted not only in the dismissal of employees but also in the abolition of certain areas of news coverage, including "women's issues," for example. This converging corporate domination and monopolization of the news creates a narrowed comprehension and tolerance for issues that involve disaffiliated and marginalized peoples. And an imminent threat of dismissal is a powerful compulsion for reporters to toe the corporate line. At the time of writing, the Department of Journalism at the University of Regina was studying the effects of this particular corporate activity, and their preliminary results suggested that certain types of media coverage were being neglected. It is easily understandable how, if such monopolization can restrict the subject matter of the news, it can also determine the editorial slant and the constructed images of good and bad. The result is that the media ultimately present the ideas and fictions of the ruling class.

These mental currencies, which are based on the ideas of superordinate people and legitimated by the media as an "objective" communicator, filter down to constrain and contain the ideas of the general reader/viewer. The constructed images of goodness and badness that we see in media portraits of young offenders become the bases of the moral framework for the entire society.

Credibility

The legitimacy of the moral framework that is created is maintained not only by the ownership of the news but also by the credibility of the news. Specifically, only a certain type of individual is accredited with the ability to comment on issues of badness and goodness. And it is no coincidence that the primary commentators in news reports are generally professional, highly educated people who are highly placed in the socio-economic system. As we saw in Chapters 3 and 4, accounts that speculate on the causes of youth crime are created and endorsed by judges, lawyers, police officers, university professors, doctors and business people. The credibility of these people results from their assumed superior knowledge and their links to science, in this case, forensic and legal science. Part of their appeal is their unique access to the exclusive languages of law and science, which, to an uninitiated public, seem mystical, inaccessible and, by definition, correct. It is also no coincidence that the legitimate speakers are drawn from the higher echelons of society. And much of their understandings of crime and punishment, as a result, are based on the values and morals of privilege. Marx's aphorism that "the ruling ideas of any age are the ideas of its ruling class" is especially powerful when we consider the socio-economic origins of "legitimate experts." Rarely are media accounts based on the insights and knowledge of marginalized or underclass people. However, the use of subverted knowledge is not an impossibility. As I show in the final chapter of this book, in one instance in which a crime account was presented through the eyes of a young street person, the vision was especially poignant and as relevant as any so-called expert opinion.

Process

The final method through which the ideas of dominant people get translated into dominating ideas is through selective media attention. Hall et al. (1978:60) argue that:

> Not every statement by a relevant primary definer in respect of a particular topic is likely to be reproduced in the media; nor is every part of each statement. By exercising selectivity the media begin to impose their own criteria on the structured "raw materials"—and thus actively appropriate and transform them. . . . [T]he criteria of selection—a mixture of professional, technical and commercial constraints—serves to orientate the media in general to the "definitions of the powerful."

On this point I would agree with the authors, and this book lends support to their thesis. The authors, however, go on to state that

> each paper's professional sense of the newsworthy, its organization and technical framework (in terms of numbers of journalists working in particular new areas, amount of column space routinely given over to certain kinds of news items, and so on), and sense of audience or regular readers, is different. Such differences, taken together, are what produce the very different "social personalities of papers." (Hall et al. 1978:60)

It is on this point that my analysis departs from the work of Hall and his associates. For, as I have argued throughout, the stories, the visual and verbal images, and the scientific accounts of youth crime are remarkably similar and constructed around a rigid set of journalistic/ideological rules. The newspapers and news magazines, with some differences in the extent of inflammatory rhetoric, could be interchanged quite easily with little change in content or intent. Hall et al. (1978) do concede, however, that, despite the different languages of newspapers, the accounts occur within certain ideological constraints. I would add that the constraints are so strong that the languages are virtually one and the same.

Conclusion

Overall, the neo-Marxist and feminist perspectives allow us to understand the entire moral panic against youth in the context of power and social control. As Steven Box argues:

> Crime and criminalization are therefore social control strategies. They: (i) render underprivileged and powerless people more likely to be arrested, convicted, and sentenced to prison, even though the amount of personal damage and injury they cause may be less than the more powerful and privileged cause; (ii) create the illusion that the "dangerous" class is primarily located at the bottom of various hierarchies by which we "measure" each other, such as occupational prestige, income level, housing market location, educational achievement, racial attributes—in this illusion it fuses relative poverty and criminal propensities and sees them both as effects of moral inferiority, thus rendering the "dangerous" class deserving of both poverty and punishment. (1983:13)

That images of poverty align with immorality and badness is manifest in media constructions, and the Marxist moral panic literature is essential in understanding the origins of hate. What are less obvious, however, are the mechanisms through which racial minorities, women and poor people get reframed in the public's mind from people who lack privilege to people who are dangerous. This is where feminist criminology, Left Realism and a Foucauldian post-modernism can help us round out a theory of the social construction of child-hating.

Chapter 7

A Kinder World for Youth

A History of Youth and Political Nihilism

As we approach the end of the millennium, there seems to be a general malaise among the Canadian population in its attitudes and orientations towards young people. As Canadian society comes to grips with the paradox of productive efficiency and social justice, it appears that we are scapegoating children while, in the process, absolving the socio-economic structure from blame for problems stemming from social inequality. Interestingly, the phenomenon of children-blaming is historically common. For example, in the seventeenth century, children, by mere virtue of their existence, were perceived to be a singular social problem. As we read this passage about life in an English town in the seventeenth century, it is remarkable how much it echoes the alarmist rhetoric in contemporary Canadian media and political accounts: the inherent danger of children, their particularly pathological vulnerability to alcohol, the importance of household discipline and "family values," and the "problem" of poverty and the reluctance of youth to become involved in wage labour.

> A large proportion of Dorchester's population thus stood in great need of reformation and discipline. One segment of them caused special concern: those of the younger generation. Noisy adolescents are always alarming to their respectable elders. And at this time there were so many of them: the product of that "baby boom" generation born after 1600. Their families were sometimes too poor to support them, they often could not or would not enter covenanted service or apprenticeship and they were always in danger of slipping outside the system of household discipline, the very foundation of social order . . . even if they were not masterless, even if they were apprenticed to respectable trades, they were always liable to be riotous and undisciplined. . . . Their drinking was a particularly serious problem. The most dangerous kind of drinking involved young people, for in their case the authority of parents or masters was obviously at risk. (Underdown 1992:79)

It is interesting, as well, how the next description of an incident of youth deviance from the same period echoes the fear of the inner city that we hear in modern accounts of crime and victimization.

> London, everyone knew, was a sink of moral iniquity far beyond the

imagination of pure-minded country folk. Be that as it may, the incident is further confirmation of the existence of a lively youth culture, a culture marked by frivolous jesting, a good deal of drinking and a keen adolescent interest in sex. . . . Apprentices being young people, their sexuality was a constant worry to their elders. . . . A paper was being passed around which Henry Follett, a dyer's apprentice, described as a catechism for women that could not hold their legs together. (Underdown 1992:82–83)

Fears of urbanism, women's sexuality and a volatile youth culture have existed in previous historical periods, just as we find them in accounts of youth crime in modern media and political discourse. It appears that youth crime was constructed rather typically at these particular periods, which were usually characterized by economic upheaval and political uncertainty. And as the reader will recall from Chapters 3 and 4, much of the disorder attributed to youth is believed to originate in poverty and womanhood as corruptions. This last passage from Underdown's book brings us up to the 1990s:

Much of the disorder that plagued Dorchester was the result of the poverty that stalked it, as it did virtually all English towns. The realities of life for the majority of people in the seventeenth century should never be forgotten: the half-starved children, the women bringing up families in grinding, unending misery, the men demoralized and driven to drink or desertion by the hopelessness of it all. . . . The able-bodied poor ought surely to be disciplined and punished for their idleness, and their children brought up in greater godliness and better work habits. . . . The desperation of the poor during this bleak year is obvious from the sharp increase in the number of cases of theft of corn that were reported. . . . Many of these cases involved women worried about the welfare of their families (1992:85–86).

Almost four hundred years later, we continue to blame able-bodied single mothers on welfare for the corruption and lack of discipline of their children, and ultimately, like in Dorchester in the seventeenth century, we blame children for idleness and for being "on the street." I present this mirror of history not to suggest that child-blaming is natural or common or justifiable. On the contrary, this replay of history shows us how socio-economic systems that have discarded certain groups of people who do not control the means of production have commonly found moral scapegoats. As they did so, social policy answers always revolved around the morality of the individual and never involved a critique of the nature of the economic system or the social order. We continue to do this in modern society and that is why it is convenient to blame children *qua* children for the ills of the world.

As we blame our children, we are confronted by a nagging contradiction to which Postman (1994) alludes in his landmark work, *The Disappearance of Childhood*. In this study of the contemporary dissolution of the distinctions between children and adults, Postman argues persuasively that the television age has forced children to confront the world of adults with all the horrific and inexplicable circumstances that that entails. He documents how the modern mass media has made it impossible for children to be isolated from the adult world and how the entertainment industry has tapped into this reality by fusing adult entertainment and the language of the adult with that of the child. This compelling argument forces us to confront the paradox and the injustice that, while we have abandoned childhood as a time of innocence and security, as our analysis of the news indicates, we preserve the category of childhood for treacherous ideological purposes. The child is the modern prototypical scapegoat, forced to live in an adult world without the rights and abilities to influence and shape that world and to defend her or his rights.

A World for Children

This book has been devoted to countering the dominant ideology in Canada with regard to youth and youth behaviour, but it is necessary to complete the polemic by demonstrating that there are child-protective and child-empowering orientations and policies that work. Unfortunately, academics—both orthodox and critical—get into a mindset that nothing works regarding crime prevention, and this mentality spills over to those who make and implement public policy. This pessimism is not only counterproductive but dangerous because it generates an apathy among public officials and youth workers that provokes ineptitude. As we have seen, this moral nihilism is fostered by sensationalist media, by alarmist politicians searching for a constituency and by fearful citizens. Further, one of the risks in advocating programs that deal with crime, deviance and dispossession is that we may be fostering more social control over already disenfranchised youth. And this is possible if school programs, for example, become so intrusive into the personal and psychic lives of youth that they become violators of human rights. However, there is no escaping the reality that many children who are the foci of society's collective wrath are forced to live on the fringes of society. It is reasonable, I think, that part of the solution to dispossession is to empower the dispossessed, both personally and politically. The programs I will describe, I believe, fulfil that mandate with minimal infringement on personal or collective rights.

The Roots of Healing

There are programs outside of Canada such as the New Zealand Family Court and the Massachusetts youth prison system closure that do provide models for change based on reacting to crime, and these programs are certainly part of the solution. In *Last One Over the Wall,* Jerome Miller (1991), the former commissioner of the Massachusetts Department of Youth Services, describes how he closed down the state's reform schools for young offenders, beginning with maximum security young inmates. The alternatives offered were based on community care, specifically community homes for young offenders, and former carceral resources were devoted to community prevention programs that provided improved education and work opportunities for underprivileged youth. After two decades, despite concerted and constant political pressure to reopen youth prisons, Massachusetts locks up fewer teenagers than any other state, its recidivism rates have dropped dramatically, the number of adult inmates who were alumni of the youth system have fallen by half, and in 1989 Massachusetts tried only twelve youths in adult court, compared to Florida, which tried more than 4,000 youths in adult court. All of this occurred with no increased risk to public safety. In fact, Massachusetts came to rank forty-sixth of the fifty states in lowest reported juvenile crimes. This astounding testimonial to the rehabilitative, community-based welfare approach, especially for maximum security offenders, suffered financial constraints in the early 1990s and there continue to be fiscal and political pressures to reopen youth jails. Never before has a grand social experiment illustrated so well how incarceration ultimately creates a more dangerous society, and yet the political detractors are powerful and influential.

New Zealand has also created a community-based youth justice system that essentially abandons the concept of incarceration to readopt a healing model for youths. Called "family group conferencing," this restorative, Maori-based model of conflict resolution was legislated under the Children, Young Persons and Their Families Act, 1989. In response to a history of high incarceration rates (second only to the United States in number of people per capita imprisoned) and a disproportionately high number of Aboriginal New Zealanders in jails, family group conferencing for youth is intended to divert children and youths from the justice system by making family conferencing mandatory for youth when criminal charges are involved. In the family group conference, the young person is confronted by the people his actions have affected. This includes the victim(s), the offender's extended family and youth justice officials. The offender is confronted by the anger of the victim(s), the responsibilities of the court system and the disappointments and anger of family members. The conference focuses on the needs of the victims and the need to have reparations made, in financial terms but more importantly in emotional terms. The philosophy of this alternative to formal, rigid justice is that the offender is given the responsibility to make things right with the victims and his or her own extended family. In the decision phase, the family deliberates in private on the course of action needed to repair the psychic and socio-economic damage and, in the vast majority of cases, the entire family group agrees on a restorative course of action that includes financial reparation and on a family-based plan to make sure the young person is held responsible and accountable while being nurtured in the family environment. Overall, the New Zealand model, based on traditional Maori cultural values, attempts to replace the punitive and retributive nature of orthodox justice with a model of restoration and healing based on the future and not on the transgressions of the past. The New Zealand model has been in operation since 1989. As of 1995, almost 95 percent of all youth cases have been resolved without court intervention, compared to 84 percent in 1993 and 55 percent in 1984. Further, there has been an 80 percent drop in youth carceral care since 1989, with no appreciable increase in the detected juvenile crime rate.

Several other international examples may be found of a non-punitive, restorative approach to youth justice. Australia has adopted an approach very much like that of New Zealand, incorporating Aboriginal values and using "talking circles" to vent anger and frustration and to ultimately reach a resolution. Japan has achieved success over a fifty-year period by employing a "communitarian" model of justice that uses community control whenever possible to make certain that the offender is not ostracized from the community through incarceration or abandonment. Like Aboriginal models of justice, the Japanese system is based on values of caring, responsibility and kinship and has progressively decreased the crime rate.

We need to look, however, no further than the boundaries of Canada for alternatives to the formal youth justice system. Mediation and alternative measures for young offenders, as mandated by the Young Offenders Act, have been used as alternatives to youth courts. The John Howard Society has for years been involved in programs that stress keeping kids out of custody and giving them opportunities whereby they can make reparation and at the same time receive counselling to restore themselves. Healing and sentencing circles are common in many Aboriginal communities in Canada and, especially in North-ern communities, are replacing the system of circuit court law that tended to "process" people with little concern for cultural and personal considerations.

For centuries, First Nations communities have dealt with antisocial behav-iour through a community well-being approach that has melded the best interests of the community with the best interests of the offender. The simple yet profound basis of this healing philosophy is that it is more appropriate and ultimately safer for society to bring offenders back into the fold than to punish or remove them from the community. When you consider that the typical repeat young offender in Canadian society is one whose past is typified by abuse and punishment, it makes little moral or practical sense to continue this abuse and punishment with legal sanctions. From a healing perspective, when someone violates the community or is punished, the community suffers collectively; the goal is to reduce violations and punishments and thus to reduce personal and collective victimization.

Unfortunately, healing is anathema to the Canadian justice system. Con-ventional law is based on authority, rank and obedience in the face of punishment. As is apparent in any study of youth at risk (or youth in contact with the law), it is this abjectly authoritarian system of unyielding obedience and punishment—in family, educational, religious, social service and court contexts—that traumatizes kids. For proof of this, one need only read any history of Aboriginal residential schools in Canada to understand how all of these contexts can actually destroy not only individuals but also cultures (cf. York 1990).

Furthermore, conventional justice does not work. As Judge Barry Stuart states:

> The state of our criminal justice system has been exposed in numerous studies. It is a mess, a very expensive mess—wasting scarce resources and tragically, needlessly wasting lives. No one, not victims, offenders, police officers, judges, not anyone working in justice can believe the justice system is just, is a "coordinated system," or is working to any measure of success in achieving its stated objectives! In many communities, evidence mounts to suggest a professional justice system not only fails to reduce crime, it contributes to the factors causing crime. (1993:283)

Aboriginal leaders in Canada, with the support and help of judges such as Barry Stuart, have lobbied to re-engage the community in dealing with issues of deviant behaviour and justice. The essence of an Aboriginal healing model is to take issues of community welfare that have been appropriated by professionals and give them back to the community. This entails the presumption that everyone is victimized by crime, including the offender, and that healing ultimately creates a safer and less offending society than does punishment. And, I would add, this same philosophy allows successful alternative school systems to work.

Community sentencing circles are based on decisions made by community members, offenders and victim(s). The high degree of consensus is based on traditional beliefs that shift the focus from solutions to crime to causes of crime. There is a growing body of material that meticulously describes the philosophy and success of sentencing circles (cf. Stuart 1993; Ross 1993; Huculak 1995; Hollow Water 1995) and I will not repeat these descriptions here except to state that, where they are practiced in well-established communities, they are relatively successful and stand in stark contrast to the unsuccessful punitive justice system currently in vogue (cf. Stuart 1993). Sentencing circles are a first step towards empowering youth and are based on restoring balance and harmony to a community. They represent only the initial stage of what I believe is a new way of approaching youth, especially youth at risk. The problem is that they still involve punishments, in the forms of banishment, reparation and conventional "rehabilitation."

Such noble initiatives, especially when applied to youth, must necessarily dispense with issues of guilt and reparation and focus on issues of human rights (including physical, psychological and social needs), privacy, mutual respect, optimism and the disappearance of the authority/obedience dyad. I am suggesting a system of youth justice similar to the system of community resolution that existed in Aboriginal cultures in Canada before industrialization and that is beginning to be restored in First Nations communities in response to centuries of privation and oppression.

Joan Ryan (1995) has produced a concise, reflective and anthropologically sensitive account of Dene traditional justice. Her research, produced through the voices of the Dene people of Lac La Marte, Northwest Territories, is an optimistic reminder that there are alternative ways of dealing with community members who break the rules that do not involve lingering guilt or punishment in the legalistic sense.

As I read accounts such as Ryan's, one thing becomes perfectly clear: effective restorative justice involves respect for individuals, the community and the physical environment. It is also perfectly obvious that in youth courts in Canada, respect is absent, from youth upwards and from legal officials downwards, and the notion of community and environment is poorly conceived in decisions regarding youth justice.

Although effective and innovative, all the above examples are necessarily reactive in their approaches to young offenders. They are intended to heal "after the fact" of the violation. In the following section, I describe education-based programs for youth that are noteworthy for several reasons. They are simple and effective; they are profound in their egalitarianism, wisdom and understanding towards disadvantaged and abused youth; and they are proactive, they reach out to the youths and the community to help personal and community healing. They are also based on a model of education that is revolutionary in relation to standardized education and in its willingness to minimize the use of authority and discipline. Most importantly, like the values inherent in traditional First Nations restorative justice models, they are based on empowering youth through the ideals and practices of respect, community and concern for the future.

The Roots of Empowerment

Princess Alexandria School

Princess Alexandria School in Saskatoon is a community-based elementary school in the inner city. The community is situated in one of the poorer areas of the city and is characterized by a relatively high transient population. Both the school and the community deal with issues typical of communities that are relegated to the margins of society, including street crime, drug and alcohol abuse and family dysfunction. Many of the students, as a result, are highly disadvantaged when they enter their school years.

The school, under the tutelage of Principal Verdyne Schmidt, has taken upon itself the task of creating a healing and nurturing environment in which violence and punishment have no place. To this end, the staff have agreed upon a philosophy of no punishment. In this environment, flexibility is the rule and not the exception, and in which acting-out is countered with options for the student, including making reparations or spending time alone. Expulsion is rarely an option. The school administrators and teachers have decided not to transfer difficult problems outside the school, as is often the case in other jurisdictions where social services or the courts are called upon to intervene. This requires a good deal of tolerance and reflection among the staff. The staff are prepared to accept verbal abuse from the kids, knowing full well that the abuse originates from traumatic life situations. They accept the axiom that children's abusive behaviour is not personal, originates outside the school context and cannot be corrected with formal, authoritarian sanction. The staff at this school either self-select or are handpicked and are aware of the needs of children who require care and nurturing beyond the three R's.

Standardized education presents a problem because it does not meet the distinctive needs of children who have not had the advantages others have. In response, the school does not "sweat the small stuff." If children do not have shoes for physical education, if they forget their books or if they are late, they are not sanctioned. A flexible curriculum allows for multigrade education, so classrooms may be homogeneous by age if not by educational level. Students are assessed on the basis of individual progress, and the concepts of pass and fail are absent from the system of assessment. Problems get solved based on the time priorities of the student and not of the school. In general, students are treated with the respect that adults are, at least formally, granted by society.

The implication of this human-rights approach to children is that the school and community are aware that, before children can be confronted with the rigours of school, they must have their physical needs met, including those for food, clothing, shelter and security, requirements that are guaranteed to all members of society. The reality of many children in this school is that their parents are struggling economically and personally and often the physical needs of the children go unmet. Thus, the school, with the help of community volunteers, begins the day with breakfast from 9:00 to 9:30, and the nutrition program continues with another hot meal during the noon period. To keep the students "off the street," recesses have been eliminated and replaced with two periods of physical education per day. Furthermore, the school provides work opportunities for older students whereby they may earn money shovelling snow or mowing grass and, in this way, buy their own clothes or feed family members if need be. Moreover, this program demonstrates the inherent goodness in children, despite the hatred and mistrust of them we see in the media. Principal Schmidt, for example, talks of instances in which an elder child has come to school out of control and verbally abusive; as the staff examine the roots of this behaviour, it is often found that the student's parents or guardians have been drinking and fighting all night, the student has had to make breakfast for his or her siblings and get them off to school and then has had to get him- or herself ready for school, all the while observing or experiencing abuse and neglect. When framed in this context, the achievements of the student are remarkable, responsible and benevolent by any standard. The school is prepared to treat such kids with the respect and tolerance they deserve, especially given their outstanding display of responsibility in the face of extreme adversity. The school, in turn, makes every effort to place siblings in the same classes or at least to provide them with opportunities to see each other, given the importance of family and caring that children often demonstrate.

The school's philosophy of mutual respect and responsibility is further demonstrated by the sense of community and sanctuary that it provides. For example, when wishing to create more communication about sensitive issues such as crime and abuse, the school meets as a community of children and adults to discuss them. When one eleven-year-old girl had been sexually assaulted outside the school, the teachers, all the children, a social worker and an elder all met to discuss issues of assault and abuse and to destigmatize the victim. The purpose of such activity is to place specific traumatic incidents in the context of general issues of safety and security and, by so doing, allow the trauma of the victim to be shared by the community. Such efforts permit the student to return to school in an atmosphere of understanding and not one of pity and fear. The school deals with issues of sexuality and sexually transmitted diseases in the same community context. Such issues are dealt with as larger social issues that involve safety, mutual respect, issues of safe sex and respect for gender, and the moral issue of blame is avoided.

The concept of community and mutual responsibility is further demonstrated by the school's reaction to vandalism. Unlike most schools, in which the caretakers and students are commonly at odds, at Princess Alexandria School the caretakers take an active part in the community of the school. They are invited to staff meetings and are involved with the education of the children. In response to vandalism, the caretakers, who live in the local community, run a Mother Earth environmental program for students that includes all aspects of ecology, including the school. The caretakers willingly give up their time on weekends to work with the students and instill in them the philosophy that the school is theirs and part of the larger environment, and that they are welcome to work with caretakers in maintaining the immediate and the larger environment. In fact, when any of the students are having a particularly bad day, they may go and work with the caretakers for a change of pace from academic pursuits.

Joe Duquette Alternative High School

Joe Duquette High School is an inner-city alternative high school in Saskatoon, Saskatchewan, whose student body is primarily of First Nations ancestry. Many of the students at the school could be said to be "high risk," in that they are disaffiliated from family and community and are relatively susceptible to confrontations with the legal system. The school is faced with issues of truancy and transience. The mandate of the school is to provide a democratic, fair environment in which students can find safety, tolerance, egalitarian treatment and a nonjudgemental, nonpunitive place to stay and learn, at least during the day.

One of the fundamental principles of the school is that the students be provided with the opportunity to make choices. And the school works at making a range of personal and academic choices available: curriculum decisions, time options including choices of term lengths and starting times, participation in cultural programs and participation in spirituality. For example, the students are not restricted to rigid guidelines about progress but are encouraged to complete studies when possible without the stigma of lagging behind. As Principal Kevin Pilon suggested, some of the students, being from backgrounds characterized by neglect and abuse, take time to overcome the trauma of life circumstances, and it is not unusual for a student like this to take three or four years to become involved in his or her own education. Healing is a timely and individual process, and this school's patience with its students reflects a profound understanding of the needs of underprivileged kids.

In essence, what the school attempts to do is create an adultlike world in which autonomy, responsibility, respect and enfranchisement are the cornerstones. To do this, the school staff creates an atmosphere of mutual respect and equality by being reflective about their own behaviour and by demonstrating respectfulness categorically; teachers demonstrate the types of conduct they expect in their students. Often, as Principal Pilon suggested, this involves admitting when they are wrong to the students, apologizing when necessary and respecting the privacy of the students against other teachers and the outside world. At times, this entails not "ratting" on a student to other teachers or the principal, and providing the school as a sanctuary against the outside, especially from the police—although the school does cooperate with the law, it does not allow the law to enter the sanctuary of the school. The atmosphere of community is fostered by a philosophy in which the school belongs to everyone; symbols of authority and "pulling rank" are minimized. To this end, the school does not have a staff room; when the staff meet, they do so in full view of the entire school community and decisions about the continuance of a student are made collectively.

Despite the fact that Joe Duquette is an innovative, community-oriented school, like all schools it necessarily has to draw the line at extreme behaviour. It does not, however, use punishment or intimidation to handle extreme situations. In cases of bullying and violence, the violating student is given a choice: either apologize and convince the victim that he or she will be safe from now on, or leave. Given that school is the only safe haven from the world and the last resort for some students, reparation is often the outcome, although expulsion does occur. In keeping with the philosophy of community and mutual investment in the school, students who are expelled are welcomed back when they are ready to accept the community standards. Once again, choice and respect, and not punishment, are the baselines.

The result of this experiment in alternative education is remarkable in many respects, although the staff remain humble about the achievements. Compared to other schools, Joe Duquette has little vandalism, little schoolyard bullying and, as the principal states, fewer behavioural problems then any school he is familiar with—all this in a student body that could be described as high-risk relative to suburban schools.

Although there are problems to overcome, the school has managed to provide a respectful, egalitarian environment in which punishment is absent and teachers are active role models for the kinds of behaviour they expect. Issues of racism, sexism and class discrimination, which are common in most schools, become subsumed under the umbrella of respect for persons as individuals and not categories. When treated like real persons, the students respond.

St. Peter's College Alternative High School

St. Peter's High School is an alternative school set in the small rural Saskatchewan community of Muenster, and it operates under the auspices of a rural school division. The school has twenty-five students of various backgrounds who are at St. Peter's because they were unable to do well in conventional classrooms. The students' disadvantages arise from socio-economic barriers, family dysfunction, scholastic problems and attendant personality problems. Like the other schools described in this chapter, its philosophy is simple yet profound. Miriam Spenrath, the principal of the school for twenty-three years, affirmed that the primary orientation towards students is to value them as individuals and to find the "gifts" that each possesses. The presumption is that each child is endowed with a variety of unique gifts and that the pursuit of lifelong learning and meaningful work is based on accessing and building upon them. The teachers believe that, if education focuses on the singular gifts of youth, the building of self-esteem occurs as a natural consequence. And, like most students in alternative programs, the students at St. Peter's High School suffer from relatively low levels of self-esteem, resulting largely from their inability to succeed in conventional education and the accompanying stigma of scholastic failure.

The focus of the school is on providing skills that the students will need to survive in the everyday world. The program focuses on teaching core curricula, but especially practical skills. Math is oriented towards personal financing, shopping, etc. English studies are directed towards providing writing, reading and verbal skills that will be required in the workplace. Students are also involved in work experience programs that expose them to at least ten different jobs. All this practical study is directed towards finding work appropriate to the special gifts and dispositions of the students, and not towards the smooth functioning of the school.

The success rate of the school is a remarkable testimony to the philosophy and the dedication of its faculty. Every student, without exception, is placed in employment upon graduation; and this occupation is, through the continued efforts of the school, appropriate to the wishes and skills of the student. These are disadvantaged students going in, so the employment success rate is even more amazing. Furthermore, when local employees hire summer students, they inquire at St. Peter's before other schools. Principal Spenrath suggests that the popularity of their students with employers is based on the attitude towards work that students acquire at the school. The school has created a twelve-point program based on the requirements of employers, which it uses to direct the work-based studies; eleven points deal with attitudes and only one addresses skills. The employers feel that skills can be taught if potential employees have positive attitudes towards work, and the success of the school is a testimony to this simple axiom.

How does the high school empower marginalized students to the point that they become preferred employees, despite the social and educational disadvantages that accompanied them when they entered? Like other successful alternative schools, the school focuses on spirituality and not on religion. The distinction is important: spirituality is based on the individual "finding" himself or herself and addressing the questions "Who am I?" and "What am I able to contribute?" To do this requires patience and considerable one-to-one interaction between students and teachers, an interaction constructed on an egalitarian "adult-to-adult" relationship. When students have bad days, as happens relatively often with disadvantaged students, the teachers spend time with them helping them through their dilemmas. Students are seldom sent to the principal's office and expulsion is rare. The only sanction is isolation, not for the purpose of punishment but for reflection. Interestingly, physical activity is used as an alternative to the classroom when students are unable to concentrate. This physical activity (typically jogging around the schoolyard) is not offered as a punishment but as a solitary time. Like the other schools I have discussed, punishment is not part of its vernacular. And students are rewarded with "incentive days," days when they are free to pursue chosen work, as a result of exemplary attendance, homework completion and positive attitude.

The other thing that strikes me about St. Peter's, and the other schools under study, is that the involvement of the community at large is vital to the student's success. The school uses to advantage its place in a small rural community, and local businesses respond with remarkable support for the school and its work programs. Business people attend the school on a regular basis not only to speak to the students but also to listen. As a consequence, they gain an understanding of the calibre, skills and attitudes of the students. Thus guesswork and uncertainty are largely eliminated before hiring. As well, the community has the opportunity to become familiar with, understand and trust students who would otherwise be considered troublemakers and miscreants. The school board, as part of the larger community, is supportive of the alternative nature of the school. Like other alternative schools, St. Peter's needs to be flexible, and standardized education is anathema to the success of such programs so a tolerant, progressive school board is vital. The community sustains its involvement by providing programs of family enrichment that address issues of violence, drug and alcohol abuse and parenting.

Like the principals at the other schools described in this chapter, Principal Spenrath talks about the resilience and remarkable diligence of her students. Several work for ten hours on the weekend and then go home and do homework for three hours. Many work all summer and display attitudes towards work rarely found among young students. The "wonderful" students described by the principal are nurtured as the result of a caring and intimate commitment by staff to provide students with the practical and psychic skills to be happy and successful. Part of this involves instilling in the student a commitment to lifelong learning, a personal orientation towards work that employers like to see, especially in a workplace that increasingly demands flexibility and continual on-the-job training.

St. Peter's High School works by providing its students with an opportunity to develop personal and occupational skills that will allow them to be preferred employees and know that they have the capability to make it in the world. The teachers are selected on the basis of their support for egalitarian and nonauthoritarian teaching. Like other successful alternative programs, the school provides an atmosphere of optimism and a context devoid of discipline and punishment. And the results are remarkable, especially given that these students would more than likely have fallen "through the cracks" in conventional schools and been "lost."

Conclusion

The schools described in this chapter have a profound understanding of the need to nurture students, especially those who are relatively disadvantaged. Punishment and the use of authority are replaced with mutual student-teacher input and mutual reflection. Students are not numbers; they are gifted individuals whose uniqueness becomes the basis of development and healing. Standardized learning is contradictory to the needs of the students and to the success of these schools. The reality is that dispossessed youth need resources to make decisions that will help them resolve their troubles and survive; more punishment cannot possibly do this.

When schools treat youth like citizens with collective and individual rights, the successes are inspiring. When I hear stories about an elementary school child who works after school to buy clothes and food for his siblings; or who, after spending a sleepless night traumatized by drunken partying and fighting by adults, gets breakfast for her siblings, makes their lunches and gets them and herself to school, albeit in a disoriented and anxious state; or who, at the age of eleven, turns a trick and shares her bounty with other children to buy things at the 7-11 (*Saskatoon Star Phoenix*, November 25, 1995:A1), I am both humbled and ashamed. I am humbled by the strength, kindness and benevolence of children, especially in dire circumstances, and ashamed by a society that fails to provide for the families and the children who live on the margins and by the venomous adult public rhetoric surrounding youth that is unfounded, false, political and patently hateful.

The solution to the distortion and demonizing at the public and political levels, as the school examples suggest, is to empower children. This suggests that the Young Offenders Act may be on the right philosophical track towards the restoration of the human rights and civil liberties of youth. However, given the individual-rights orientation of law, the collective needs of youth are difficult to ensure, especially under the Charter of Rights and Freedoms. Good schools, however, seem to blend individual and collective rights well. Maybe the Charter and the YOA need to go further and extend rights to children as an identifiable collective. This may, for example, redefine the public attack on children described in this book as a form of hate literature, unacceptable both legally and morally.

This excerpt from the *Saskatoon Star Phoenix* (April 4, 1996:A5) is an example of what we could report about kids and is also a reminder that society is terribly mistaken in its attitudes and practices towards children.

Street Kids Gather in Search of Family Love
by Kenneth Noskiye

When I was 15, I lived on the streets of Edmonton in the area known as "The Drag." I don't know why they called it that. Maybe it was because people got dragged into the areas by the drugs and the so-called fast life, which usually meant a fast death.

I ran into a group of other young people who hung out in the same area. We became known as the "Boyle Street Kids."

The aboriginal kids usually came from the northern parts of Alberta and Saskatchewan. Most of the non-aboriginal kids were runaways.

It was a struggle to survive.

Getting food wasn't too much of a problem. We figured out pretty fast where the food kitchens were. Church groups, bless their hearts, would also come onto the streets with food and vitamins.

Some of us tried to find jobs but we were all too young to work. So, we turned to the only source of income we could find: running drugs for the pushers. They wouldn't let any of us sell drugs, probably scared we would take over their markets. We ran drugs from the seller to the buyer. Of course, this made it safer for the drug dealers.

We used to wait outside hotels as the dealer inside was making a deal. When the trade was made, the dealer would tell us and we would make the transfer.

The girls in our group would scout for a "mark." It's really amazing how many men—usually middle-aged and white—would come down to The Drag flashing all kinds of money. When a target was found, we would make plans to get his money.

Violent robbery was the last resort. What usually worked was to get the guy to think he was going to have sex with one of the young girls, add alcohol and drugs and the next thing you knew he was passed out, with no money, no watch, no ring, no vehicle. And—if they were nice enough and they fit—no clothes.

The girls, all around my age, were not allowed to work as prostitutes. This rule was enforced not by us, not by the law and not by the older prostitutes, but by the pimps.

I knew prostitutes who weren't scared of anything. They weren't scared of the police, the perverted johns or any other prostitute. But, the pimps sent chills up their spines.

The pimps allowed us to hang around because we attracted the johns.

We always had to be careful about the perverts who drove around and around the block like clockwork. Sometimes, they would pull over and ask one of us, usually a boy, to come with them. Any boy who went with a john was rarely seen afterward. Probably, he was too ashamed for what the john made him do.

The police were about our only friends. They used us to keep track of the johns, especially those who asked for kids.

We got to know the police on a first-name basis. One time, a cop picked us up, about 10 of us. We thought we were getting arrested. Instead, he took us to a football game. The Eskimos kicked ass that day. We cheered.

That was almost 20 years ago.

Today, when I hear stories about street kids, I am saddened. I hate hearing the streets glamorized, like it was some kind of "NYPD Blue" television show. It's kids trying to survive the only way they know how.

The worst part is when I hear people who think they know all the answers from the warmth of their homes blame the parents of street kids. Most of the kids don't even know where their parents are.

These people blame the police for not doing anything, when the police are sometimes the only people the kids turn to for help. They blame outreach workers, who work endlessly for the kids.

I get unsettled when I hear a politician say, "We have to get tough," knowing perfectly well politicians are sometimes a prostitute's best customers.

Just before I turned 16, I was walking by myself. It was raining. I stopped at a house and stood under a porch to escape the rain. I looked through the window.

I saw a family watching television, eating popcorn and having fun together. I stood there and wished not for a car, not for a million dollars, not for a mansion to live in. I wished I had a family, someone to care and love me.

I walked away, back into the rain, back to the only family I knew, the street kids!

All they're trying to do is survive.

Bibliography

Alberta Report. 1995. "Vietnamese Are Blamed for Recent Calgary School Violence." January 2:28.

———. 1995. "You've come a long way, baby: Prodded by feminism, today's teenaged girls embrace antisocial male behaviour." July 31:24.

———. 1994. "Two Are Stronger than One: Alberta Teens from Traditional Families Are Less Drug Prone." May 2:38.

———. 1994. "Junior gone wild: An aging do-your-own-thing generation lashes out at its savage offspring." May 9:37.

———. 1993. "The Horror World of 'Mattress Girls': Child Prostitution is Not Unique to Asians, Police Insist." October 17:28.

———. 1993. "I Am Gavin: How a bright kid with excellent self-esteem slaughtered his whole family." December 6:18.

———. 1993. "Crimes Beyond Reason." December 6:20.

———. 1992. "The Crooked Credit Card Capital: Calgary Police Blame Surging Fraud on the City's Asian Gangs." September 21:22.

———. 1992. "New Insights into Alberta's Asian Crime Scene: The Publicity Angers Edmonton's Viets, But Police Say People Have to Know How Extensive It Is." October 26:22.

Anderson, Margaret. 1988. *Thinking About Women: Sociological Perspectives on Sex and Gender.* New York: Macmillan.

Balbus, Isaac 1973. *Dialectics of Repression.* New York: Russell Sage Foundation.

Becker, Howard S. 1963. *Outsiders: Studies in the Sociology of Deviance.* New York: Free Press.

Box, Steven. 1987. *Recession, Crime and Punishment.* Totowa, N.J.: Barnes and Noble.

———. 1983. *Power, Crime, and Mystification.* New York: Tavistock.

Bradley, Ann. 1994. "A Morality Play for Our Times." *Living Marxism* (January):10–13.

Calgary Herald. 1995. "Moms Furious at MLA's Betrayal: Tory Calls Single Mothers Vindictive Leeches." April18:A2.

———. 1995. "Teen Violence: Murder, Mayhem have their Roots in Boredom." April 18:A5.

———. 1992. "Kids next door could be violent." May 11:A1, A2.

———. 1990. "Neglected Kids Kill More Than Time: Violent Youth Offences Rising Fast in Canada." August 9:C3.

Cantor, D., and K.C. Land. 1985. "Unemployment and Crime Rates in the Post-World War II United States: A Theoretical and Empirical Analysis." *American Sociological Review* (50):317–32.

Carrigan, D. Owen. 1991. *Crime and Punishment in Canada: A History.* Toronto: McClelland and Stewart.

Carrington, P. 1995. "Has Violent Crime Increased? Comment on Corrado and Markwart." *Canadian Journal of Criminology* (37):61–74.

Chambliss, William. 1969. *Crime and the Legal Process.* New York: McGraw-Hill.

Chatelaine. 1993. "Teenage Mutant Ninja Canadians." May:74, 75.

Cohen, Stanley. 1985. *Visions of Social Control.* Toronto: Polity Press.

————. 1980 Folk Devils *and Moral Panics: The Creation of the Mods and Rockers.* Second edition. New York: St. Martin's Press.

Comack, Elizabeth. 1991. "'We will get some good out of this riot yet:' The Canadian State, Drug Legislation and Class Conflict." In Elizabeth Comack and Stephen Brickey (eds.), *The Social Basis of Law: Critical Readings in the Sociology of Law.* Halifax: Garamond Press.

Currie, Dawn. 1991. "Realist Criminology, Women and Social Transformation in Canada." In Brian MacLean and Dragan Milovanovic (eds.), *New Directions in Critical Criminology.* Vancouver: Collective Press.

Daily Mail. 1993. November 25. In Bradley, Ann. 1994. "A Morality Play for our Times." Livi*ng Marxism* (January):12.

Earls, C.P., and H. David. 1990. "Early Family Sexual Experiences of Male and Female Prostitutes." *Canada's Mental Health* (December):7–11.

Elliot, D.S., and S. Ageton. 1980. "Reconciling Race and Class Differences in Self-Reported and Official Estimates of Delinquency." *American Sociological Review* 45:95–110.

Foucault, Michel. 1980. *Michel Foucault: Power and Knowledge.* London: Harvester Wheatsheaf.

Gartner, R., and A. Doob. 1994. "Trends in Criminal Victimization 1988–93." J*uristat Service Bulletin, CCJS* 14(13).

Gelsthorpe, Loraine, and Allison Morris. 1990. *Feminist Perspectives in Criminology.* Buckingham, U.K.: Open University Press.

Globe and Mail. 1992. Youth Violence: An Unsettling Trend." November 19:A8.

————. 1990. "Youth Gang Violence on Rise: Toronto Schools, Police Urge Community to Act." May 23:A1, A2.

Goff, Colin, and Charles Reasons. 1978. *Corporate Crime in Canada.* Toronto: Prentice-Hall.

Goode, Erich, and Nachman Ben-Yehuda. 1994. *Moral Panics: The Social Construction of Deviance.* Oxford: Blackwell.

Green, Melvyn. 1986. "The History of Canadian Narcotics Control: The Formative Years." In Neil Boyd (ed.), *The Social Dimensions of Law.* Scarborough, Ont.: Prentice-Hall.

Hackett, Robert A. 1991. *News and Dissent: The Press and the Politics of Peace in Canada.* Norwood, N.J.: Ablex.

Hale, C. 1989. "Economy, Punishment and Imprisonment." *Contemporary Crises* 13:327–49.

Hall, Stuart, Chas Critcher, Tony Jefferson, John Clarke and Brian Roberts. 1978. *Policing the Crisis: Mugging, the State and Law and Order.* London: Macmillan.

Hamilton, A.C., and C.M. Sinclair, 1991. *Report of the Aboriginal Justice Inquiry of Manitoba. Volume 1: The System and Aboriginal People.* Winnipeg: Queen's Printer.

Herman, Edward S., and Noam Chomsky. 1988. *Manufacturing Consent: The Political Economy of the Mass Media.* New York: Pantheon.

Hollow Water. 1995. "Interim Report of the Hollow Water First Nations Community Holistic Circle Healing." *Justice as Healing: A Newsletter on Aboriginal Concepts of Justice* (Winter):7–8.

Huculak, Judge Brian. 1995. "From the Power to Punish to the Power to Heal." *Justice as Healing: A Newsletter on Aboriginal Concepts of Justice.* Saskatoon: Native

Law Centre, University of Saskatchewan.

Hunt, Alan. 1991. "Postmodernism and Critical Criminology." In Brian MacLean and Dragan Milovanovic (eds.), *New Directions in Critical Criminology*. Vancouver: Collective Press.

Iyengar, Shanto, and Donald R. Kinder. 1987. *News That Matters*. Chicago: University of Chicago Press.

Jenkins, Philip. 1992. *Intimate Enemies: Moral Panics in Contemporary Britain*. New York: Aldine de Gruyter.

Kaihla, Paul, John DeMont and Chris Wood. 1994. "Kids Who Kill: Special Report." *Maclean's* (August 15):32–39.

Kappeler, Victor E., Mark Blumberg and Gary W. Potter. 1993. *The Mythology of Crime and Delinquency*. Prospect Heights, Ill.: Waveland Press.

Kellner, Douglas. 1995. "Cultural Studies, Multiculturalism and Media Culture." In Gail Dines and Jean M. Humez (eds.), *Gender, Race and Class in Media: A Text Reader*. Thousand Oaks, Calif.: Sage.

Kershaw, A., and M. Lasovich. 1991. *Rock-A-Bye Baby: A Death Behind Bars*. Toronto: McClelland and Stewart.

LaPrairie, Carol Pitcher. 1988. "The Young Offenders Act and Aboriginal Youth." In Joe Hudson, Joseph Hornick and Barbara Burrows (eds.), *Justice and the Young Offender in Canada*. Toronto: Wall and Thompson.

LeBlanc, M. 1983. "Delinquency as an Epiphenomenon of Adolescence." In R. Corrado, M. Leblanc and J. Trepanier (eds.), *Current Issues in Juvenile Justice*. Toronto: Butterworths.

Lowman, J. 1991. "Understanding Prostitution in Canada. An Evaluation of the Brannigan-Fleischman Opportunity Model." *Canadian Journal of Law and Society* 6:13–64.

———. 1989 *Street Prostitution: Assessing the Impact of the Law (Vancouver)*. Ottawa: Minister of Justice and Attorney General of Canada, Department of Justice.

Lowman, J., and B. MacLean. 1992. *Realist Criminology: Crime Control and Policing in the 1990s*. Toronto: University of Toronto Press.

MacLean, B., and D. Milovanovic. 1991. *New Directions in Critical Criminology*. Vancouver: Collective Press.

Maclean's. 1992. "The Young Offender: A Wave of Teenage Crime Shocks Ottawa." May 18:35.

Massumi, Brian, ed. 1993. *The Politics of Everyday Fear*. Minneapolis: University of Minnesota Press.

McCormick, Chris. 1995. *Constructing Danger: The Mis/Representation of Crime in the News*. Halifax: Fernwood.

McLuhan, Marshall. 1964. *Understanding Media: The Extensions of Man*. New York: McGraw-Hill.

Miller, Jerome. 1991. *Last One Over the Wall: The Massachusetts Experiment in Closing Reform Schools*. Columbus: Ohio State University Press.

Montreal Gazette. 1993. "About 30 Kids a Year Charged with Murder." July 18:C1.

———. 1991. July 18:C1. [need title]

———. 1989. "Kid Gloves Treatment: YOA Has Been Accused of Letting Juveniles Get Away with Murder." April 8:B1. ***check

Monture-Angus, Patricia. 1996. *Thunder in My Soul: A Mohawk Woman Speaks*. Halifax: Fernwood.

Painter, Kate. 1993. "The Mythology of Delinquency: An Empirical Critique." Paper presented at the British Criminology Conference, Cardiff University.

Platt, Anthony. 1969. *The Child Savers: The Invention of Delinquency.* Chicago: University of Chicago Press.

Postman, Neil. 1994. *The Disappearance of Childhood.* New York: Vintage.

———. 1988. *Conscientious Objections: Stirring Up Trouble About Language, Technology, and Education.* New York: Alfred A. Knopf.

———. 1985. *Amusing Ourselves to Death: Public Discourse in the Age of Show Business.* New York: Penguin.

Poulantzas, Nicos. 1972. "The Problem of the Capitalist State." In Robin Blackburn (ed.), *Ideology in the Social Sciences.* New York: Pantheon.

Quinney, Richard. 1974. *Critique of Legal Order: Crime Control in Capitalist Society.* Boston: Little, Brown.

Ramazanoglu, Caroline. 1993. *Up Against Foucault: Explorations of Some Tensions Between Foucault and Feminism.* London: Routledge.

Reid-MacNevin, Susan. 1991. "A Theoretical Understanding of Current Canadian Juvenile-justice Policy." In Alan Leschied, Peter Jaffe and Wayne Willis (eds.), *The Young Offenders Act: A Revolution in Canadian Juvenile Justice.* Toronto: University of Toronto Press.

Rosenau, Pauline M. 1992. *Postmodernism and the Social Sciences—Insights, Inroads, and Intrusions.* Princeton, N.J.: Princeton University Press.

Ross, Rupert. 1995. "Aboriginal Community Healing in Action: The Hollow Water Approach." *Justice as Healing: A Newsletter on Aboriginal Concepts of Justice.* Saskatoon: Native Law Centre, University of Saskatchewan.

———. 1993. *Dancing with a Ghost: Exploring Indian Reality.* Markham, Ont.: Octopus.

Ryan, Joan. 1995. *Doing Things the Right Way: Dene Traditional Justice in Lac La Marte, N.W.T.* Calgary: University of Calgary Press.

Ryan, William. 1976. *Blaming the Victim.* New York: Vintage.

Saskatoon Star Phoenix. 1996. "Street Kids Gather in Search of Family Love." April 4:A5.

———. 1995. "Street Gangs Reality in City." November 4:A1, A2.

———. 1995. "Community Said Vital to Fighting Street Gangs." December 2:A8.

———. 1994. "Murder suspect found in pool of blood." August 31:D12.

———. 1989. "Youths treat crime as joke." May 31:A6.

Schissel, Bernard. 1995a. "Trends in Official Crime Rates." In James Creechan and Robert Silverman (eds.), *Canadian Delinquency.* Scarborough, Ont.: Prentice-Hall.

———. 1995b. "Degradation, Social Deprivation and Violence: Health Risks for Women Prisoners." In B. Singh Bolaria and Rosemary Bolaria (eds.), *Women, Medicine and Health.* Halifax: Fernwood.

———. 1993. The *Social Dimensions of Canadian Youth Justice.* Don Mills, Ont.: Oxford University Press.

———. 1992. "The influence of economic factors and social control policy on crime rate changes in Canada, 1962–1988." *Canadian Journal of Sociology* 17(4):405–28.

Shaver, Fran. 1993. "Prostitution: A Female Crime?" In E. Adelberg and C. Currie (eds.), *In Conflict with the Law: Women and the Canadian Justice System.*

Vancouver: Press Gang.

Smart, Carol. 1990. "Feminist Approaches to Criminology or Postmodern Women Meets Atavistic Man." In Loraine Gelsthorpe and Allison Morris (eds.), *Feminist Perspectives in Criminology*. Buckingham, U.K.: Open University Press.

Snyder, Howard N., and Melissa Sickmund. 1995. *Juvenile Offenders and Victims: A National Report*. Washington, D.C.: Office of Juvenile Justice and Delinquency Prevention.

Statistics Canada. 1992. "Violent Youth Crime." *Canadian Social Trends* 26:2–9.

Stuart, Judge Barry. 1993. "Community-Based Justice Initiatives: An Overview." *Seeking Common Ground*. Publication from the 21st International Conference, Society of Professionals in Dispute Resolution (SPIDR). Toronto: SPIDR.

Underdown, David. 1992. *Fire from Heaven: Life in an English Town in the Seventeenth Century*. London: Harper Collins.

Vancouver Sun. 1994. "Asian Not Dominant Force in Youth Gangs, New Study Stresses." February 3:B1.

———. 1993. "Defiance of the Law Brings Claim Young Offenders Act Too Limited: It's Outrageous Behaviour by Outrageous Children Probably Raised by Outrageous Parents." April 16:A4.

———. 1992. "Teen violence is on the rise." September 19:A1.

———. 1987. "Delinquency Predictable by the Age of 8." February 26:9.

West, Gordon. 1991. "Towards a More Socially Informed Understanding of Canadian Delinquency Legislation." In Alan Leschied, Peter Jaffe and Wayne Willis (eds.), *The Young Offenders Act: A Revolution in Canadian Juvenile Justice*. Toronto: University of Toronto Press.

———. 1984. *Young Offenders and the State: A Canadian Perspective on Delinquency*. Toronto: Butterworths.

Western Report. 1992. "A generation of outlaws: Wildly rising teen crime is blamed on a molly-coddle law." February 24:18–19.

———. 1992. "Youth Crime and Coddling: The new act won't mean tougher sentences, police say, so the mayhem will continue." May 4:22.

———. 1992. "The age outside the law: Three young boys turn a town upside down and nobody can touch them." August 31:25.

———. 1991. "Coping with Criminals: A Plague of Teen Crime Illustrates the Failure of the Young Offenders Act." April 15:45.

Winnipeg Free Press. 1994. "Angry, Bitter Kids Flex Their Muscles: An Outsider's Guide to Youth Gangs." September 29:B1.

———. 1994. "Bad Boys . . . All Know Gunshot Victims." October 3:B2.

———. 1993. "Liverpool: A Tinder-Box." March 18:D11.

———. 1993. "Teen Gangs Attractive to Students." April 14:B2, B8.

Winterdyk, John A. 1996. "Trends and Patterns in Youth Crime." In John Winterdyk (ed.), *Issues and Perspectives on Young Offenders in Canada*. Toronto: Harcourt Brace.

York, Geoffrey. 1990. *The Dispossessed: Life and Death in Native Canada*. Toronto: Little, Brown.

Related titles
from Fernwood Publishing

WOMEN IN TROUBLE

Connecting Women's Law Violation to their Histories of Abuse

Elizabeth Comack (Manitoba)

This book addresses one of the more alarming findings to emerge about women in prison: the fact that 80 percent report histories of physical and sexual abuse.

"Elizabeth allows the women in this book to speak their own truth. It's a graphic, shocking, depressing and absolutely necessary account of the connections between histories of abuse and trouble with the law." —Karen Toole-Mitchell, *Winnipeg Free Press*

150pp Paper ISBN 1 895686 61 X $14.95

CONSTRUCTING DANGER

The Mis/Representation of Crime in the News

Chris McCormick

This book examines different criminal topics through looking at actual news articles and analyzing how subtle distortions creep into crime coverage. The underlying perspective is that the news not only reports crime but socially constructs it, reproducing crime myths in the process.

234pp Paper ISBN 1 895686 45 8 $19.95

THUNDER IN MY SOUL

A Mohawk Woman Speaks

Patricia Monture-Angus (Saskatchewan)

This book contains the reflections of one Mohawk woman and her struggles to find a good place to be in Canadian society. The essays, written in enjoyable and accessible language, document the struggles against oppression that Aboriginal people face, as well as the success and change that have come to Aboriginal communities. It speaks to both the mind and the heart.

273pp Paper ISBN 1 895686 46 6 $19.95

New and recent Basics
from Fernwood Publishing

The Basics present topics of current interest—many on the cutting edge of scholarship—in a short and inexpensive format that makes them ideal as supplementary texts and for general interest. New proposals for the series are welcome.

CRIMES, LAWS, AND COMMUNITIES
John L. McMullan, David C. Perrier, Peter D. Swan, Stephen Smith
In this book, McMullan and his colleagues have provided much needed information and analysis on "unconventional" crimes by researching fire for profit, illegal fishing and business crime in Atlantic Canada. The three essays fill an information gap left by scant media reports, conflicting government statistics and, in the case of crimes of capital, wilfully concealed information.
Contents: Going to Blazes: The Social Economy of Arson • Poaching vs. the Law: The Social Organization of Illegal Fishing • Toxic Steel: Corporate Crime and the Contamination of the Environment
112pp Paper ISBN 1 895686 79 2 $12.95

IMMIGRATION AND THE LEGALIZATION OF RACISM
Lisa Jakubowski
"The chameleon-like nature of the law—the duplicitous ways in which the law is written, the equivocal way in which it is stated and, therefore, talked about, the hiding of the truth about the resources which are expended in its implementation, the misleading way in which it casts the discretions it purports to take away and to give—its ideological functioning and its capacity to legitimate the illegitimate, all are put under the microscope in this study. It is a timely piece of work. It may make some readers uncomfortable, but it will leave no one untouched." —*H.J Glasbeek, Professor Emeritus, Osgoode Hall Law School*
Contents: Controlling Immigration: "Race" and Canadian Immigration Law and Policy Formation • The Question of Social Order: Exploring the Duality of Law • Ideology as Methodology: Documentary Analysis of Canadian Immigration Law • Amending the Canadian Immigration Act: The Live-In Caregiver Program • Amending the Canadian Immigration Act: Bill C-86 • Concluding Remarks
116pp Paper ISBN 1 895686 74 1 $12.95

POLITICS OF COMMUNITY SERVICES
Immigrant Women, Class and the State (Second edition)
Roxana Ng
"Students like it a lot. It is readable, although it offers a complex argument. It is practical and speaks to experiences that many [students] have had. It offers a model of what an empirical study using social organization of knowledge looks like." —*Marie Campbell, Social Work, University of Victoria*
110pp Paper ISBN 1 895686 64 4 $12.95

POLITICS ON THE MARGINS
Restructuring and the Canadian Women's Movement
Janine Brodie
"Janine Brodie's thoughtful and insightful analysis of the impact of international restructuring on the women's movement asks all the right questions. Her challenge to develop new strategies in the face of the destruction of the welfare state should be taken up by feminists everywhere." —*Judy Rebick*
120pp Paper ISBN 1 895686 47 4 $12.95

ELUSIVE JUSTICE
Beyond the Marshall Inquiry
Joy Mannette ed. (York)
"The Marshall Commission Report does not deserve accolades. While it acknowledges errors, negligence and mismanagement, it did not make the connections necessary to begin the process of developing a dialogue about a justice system that Aboriginal people can respect, or which respects Aboriginal people." —*M.E. Turpel, Dalhousie Law School*
108pp Paper ISBN 1 895686 02 4 $12.95

MAN'S WILL TO HURT
Investigating the Causes, Supports and Varieties of His Violence
Joseph A. Kuypers (Manitoba)
This book identifies how men code their will to hurt to make it moral, and how they ignore the drastic realities of excessive male violence.
127pp Paper ISBN 1 895686 06 7 $12.95